WITHDRAWN
NDSU

BARRETT H. CLARK

THE
CONTINENTAL DRAMA OF TO-DAY

Outlines for Its Study By BARRETT H. CLARK

Suggestions, questions, biographies, and bibliographies with outlines, of half a dozen pages or less each, of the more important plays of Ibsen, Björnsen, Strindberg. Tolstoy, Gorky, Tchekoff, Andreyeff, Hauptmann, Sudermann, Wedekind, Schnitzler, Von Hoffmansthal, Becque, Le Maître, Lavedan, Donnay, Maeterlinck, Rostand, Hervieu, Giacosa, D'Annunzio, Echegaray, and Galdós. While intended to be used in connection with a reading of the plays themselves, the book has an independent interest. 12 mo. $1.50 net.
(Published by HENRY HOLT AND COMPANY, New York)

"Three Modern Plays from the French,"
THE PRINCE D'AUREC, THE PARDON,
THE OTHER DANGER

Translated by Barrett H. Clark, with an introduction by Clayton Hamilton. 12 mo. Net $1.35.
(Published by HENRY HOLT AND COMPANY, New York)

THE LABYRINTH

A play in five acts, by Paul Hervieu. Authorized translation by Barrett H. Clark and Lander MacClintock. 16 mo. Net $1.00.
(Published by B. W. HUEBSCH, New York)

FOUR PLAYS OF THE FREE THEATER

The Fossils *By François de Curel*
The Serenade *By Jean Jullien*
Françoise' Luck *By Georges de Porto-Riche*
The Dupe *By Georges Ancey*

PRODUCED AT THE THÉÂTRE LIBRE

Translated with an Introduction

BY

BARRETT H. CLARK

Preface by Brieux of the French Academy

CINCINNATI
STEWART & KIDD COMPANY
1915

Copyright, 1914, by
STEWART & KIDD COMPANY
All Rights Reserved
Copyright in England

First impression November, 1914

14-21621

PQ
1240
E8
C5

VAIL-BALLOU COMPANY
BINGHAMTON AND NEW YORK

CONTENTS

Engl. & Lit.
Benson
17-D.-'30
48273

PREFACE

MR. BARRETT H. CLARK,
Berlin,

My Dear Colleague:

The Nineteenth Century was an age which strove in the pursuit of truth; during the last twenty years that struggle became strikingly manifest, for the theater itself was affected.

After the stupidities of Romanticism — with its moonlit fortresses and factitious medievalism, its poniards and poison-vials, its caverns and towers, its châtelaines and sorcerers, its murders and idle gossip, men began to feel the need of a closer observation of the life about them. After a period of narrow philosophic spirituality, there arose the desire to examine with a critical eye that which in the past had been accepted as a matter of course. Science, which was the heritage of the Nineteenth Century, rapidly became "experimental."

As the French temperament was fertile ground for the new ideas, beautiful plants and flowers and great trees sprang up with a vigor which seemed wholly spontaneous.

In the realm of philosophy it was Taine, in medicine Claude Bernard, in science all the Positivists, who paved the way for the new literature. Balzac was the first. His work marks the transition between Romanticism and Naturalism.

In him are the defects of exaggeration of both schools. Certain conceptions and ideas of his are at times childishly, monstrously distorted, sufficiently so to rank him with the worst of his predecessors, while at other times again he thinks and writes with a power so violent and so audacious, that none of his disciples has been able to equal him — in spite of the fact that every follower is prone to exaggerate the manner of his master. Zola was to follow, however.

The theater — if we except certain plays of that true precursor of the moderns, Émile Augier, and the occasionally inspired priests of Dumas *fils* — was confined rigidly within certain time-honored conventions, and lay like a lazybones in a warm and comfortable bed. The theaters of Paris all had their accepted and privileged purveyors of amusement, and their intellectual sloth was in turn communicated to the public — each supporting the other.

Yet a deep-buried desire for something new existed somewhere in the mind of the public; it was latent, unknown, unconscious — but it was so real, so sincere, that when the first attempts to bring the theater into a closer relation with life were brought to the stage, these were greeted with cries of joy and enthusiasm.

It is Antoine's chief glory to have felt this desire, to have been the first to bring it to its full fruition. From the moment he made his appearance, in the obscure little theater in the Passage de l'Elysée des Beaux-arts, dramatists brought him plays in which they too had endeavored to do away with the old conventions, and in which they tried to affect the men and women of their day through sincere work reflecting more clearly than ever before the life of their time. All these authors *existed,* no doubt, but their works were not produced, their manuscripts were not even read, and it is not difficult to believe that many of them would have faltered and failed in the face of everlasting discouragement, had it not been for Antoine who, while not advertising them nor exploiting them, merely "placed" them, made them feel that they existed, and helped them to realize their individuality. Without attempting to guide or directly influence them, his powerful personality made itself felt even with the strongest-willed and most independent of his co-workers. His unruffled good humor in the face of the protestations called down upon his head by the new-school dramatists, his faith in himself and in his work, his manner of accepting the most patent defeat as the most brilliant of victories, his admirable fighting spirit, his courage — all this, and other things besides — made of the little band which constituted the original Théâtre Libre, a living company, an insolent band of enthusiasts even, an enemy of tinsel and false glory (and at times, it must be confessed, of true glory, for it was occasionally extreme in its attitude) but always ready for a struggle, valiant in the cause of truth, of beauty, of poverty, of independence: fanatical and brutal, too. In a word, it possessed those qualities which attract and hold the attention of the people at large.

Antoine was fortunate as a revolutionary in that he was not in the least exclusive. By personal inclination and taste he believed in a realistic expression of life, yet his enthusiasm for the " play of ideas " attracted him to François de Curel, and for the love and sex drama to Georges de Porto-Riche.

I remember — with what a thrill! — the many pleasant and inspiring evenings I have spent in the company of these enthusiasts. Pitiless like all neophytes, violent as well, each of us was a sort of Polyeucte, eager to smash the idols of the past.

The influence of the Théâtre Libre upon the development of the theater in France was enormous. Even those who opposed it most bitterly, tried later to imitate it, but as they lacked Faith, that divinely essential Faith, they succeeded in imitating only the technical *methods:* they were capable only of copying what was of least value and. in the apt words of Jules Lemaître, the result was a " nouveau poncif "—" a re-hashing of stale material."

Now Antoine — who would believe it? — Antoine is a timid man. You may take the word of one who has known him intimately for a quarter of a century. In the early days Antoine was seized with fear in the presence of an audience. Those thousand pairs of eyes, often enough full of mockery, at times distinctly hostile, were the source of much uneasiness to the young actor. I must add that at times there was imposed on him the difficult task of flinging in the teeth of that public expressions which were particularly daring and odious. Then, in order to escape the gaze of that multitude, he instinctively turned round one day, and continued to speak his lines, his back turned to the footlights. That seemed to cap the climax. At the

Comédie Française, the temple of dramatic conventions, I know one Théâtre Libre dramatist who was once very much irritated because the actors, wishing to please him, rehearsed with their backs turned *continually* to the audience!

Antoine's work produced more important and lasting results. He it was who for the first time introduced to the public a large number of dramatists hitherto unknown, many of whom it is certain would otherwise never have had a hearing. He was the first to bring Ibsen to France, and François de Curel into international renown. Antoine showed us greater and finer possibilities in staging, his *mise en scène* constituted a revolt against the old-fashioned stage-sets, many of which seemed an insult to the artistic sensibilities of the spectator. He reduced the number of stage conventions, he encouraged and successfully produced the works of new authors, and taught the general public to look for and appreciate dramatic work of better quality and nobler inspiration than that to which it had as a rule been accustomed.

It is not his fault if the public is but rarely offered an opportunity to develop that better taste which he did so much to improve, and which at times seems likely to disappear for want of sufficient nutriment!

BRIEUX.

SONNET À ANTOINE

" Le théâtre ? " me disiez-vous au coin de l'âtre ;
" Travail de fou dans la poussière . . . Espoirs
. . . Dégoût . . .
Pauvreté des moyens . . . On crie, on rage, on
bout . . .
Çà n'y est pas! . . . C'est du carton et c'est du
plâtre ! "

Et puis, un souffle passe . . . et c'est un coin
bleuâtre
Où, pendant un instant, *çà y est,* tout d'un coup !
Et c'est ça,— cet instant qui console de tout,—
" C'est çà," me disiez-vous, Antoine, " le théâ-
tre ! "

La Vie aussi, mon cher ami. Ce n'est que pour
Deux ou trois beaux instants de victoire ou
d'amour
Que le Héros reprend sans fin sa tentative.

Soit ! Vous la reprendrez demain, grand obstiné !
Mais un de ces instants qui valent que l'on vive,
Je crois bien que, ce soir, Paris vous l'a donné !

EDMOND ROSTAND

ANTOINE AND THE "FREE THEATER"

The "Free Theater" was to the French drama of the past quarter century what the Reformation was to Christianity; André Antoine was its Martin Luther. Like Luther, this energetic Frenchman did not originate or invent his revolution, he merely happened to live at a time when revolt was in the air: both brought to a head a number of symptoms and eventually formulated the ideas of their time and fixed for future generations those ideas which each had found and developed. To Antoine it appeared that the drama of his day was fettered with conventions of style, technic, and subject-matter to such an extent that young dramatists with new ideas and new ways of expressing them, had little or no opportunity to produce their works. The founding of his little troupe of amateurs was a declaration of independence from the "well-made" plays of Scribe and his followers. The experiment was so successful that within less than ten years it ceased to be of use, and died of inertia. The forces Antoine was combatting gave way before him, so that within less than twenty years he found that as director of the Odéon Theater — surely one of the most conventional of Parisian playhouses! — he was able to mount what plays he pleased and in what manner seemed best to him.

The nineteenth century was one of the most fertile periods in the history of the French stage. Beginning with the Romanticists — Victor Hugo, Dumas père, Alfred de Vigny — contemporaneous with the "Vaudevillistes," dominated by the commanding Scribe, there arose two of the most original and revolutionary of modern dramatists: Alexandre Dumas fils and Émile Augier. They were the originators of the social "thesis" play. The individual in conflict with society and conventions was what interested these moralists; their influence was later to be observed in the works of Ibsen who, it will be seen, in turn contributed largely to the ideas of the younger writers of Antoine's movement. Yet the general trend of the nineteenth century was toward the presentation of life molded into a more or less conventional form. The school of Scribe, in which Victorien Sardou was the greatest scholar, has furnished models of technic which have remained to this day.

At rare intervals there arose a dramatist who endeavored to get a little closer to life, delve a little deeper into human motives and paint with a defter hand the manners of his day. Balzac, trying to carry into the realm of the theater some of that marvelous power of observation which is the chief glory of his masterpieces of fiction, wrote one play which was a forerunner of the Antoine movement: "Mercadet" is undeniably crude, yet its very crudity lends an air of actuality to it which is lacking even in some of the best plays of Dumas fils and Augier. Another novelist, later in the century, turned to the theater: Zola's "Thérèse Raquin" is a tragedy of remorse, which was to exercise considerable influence over the younger generation. At a time when the stage was dominated by conventions, Henry Becque had the good fortune to have his two masterpieces, "Les Corbeaux" and "La Parisienne" ("The Vultures" and "The Woman of Paris") produced; these uncompromising and occasionally brutal pictures, especially the former, constitute, in the words of James Huneker, the Bible of the Naturalist School of drama. With a profound contempt for formula and accepted tradition, for every trick of the trade, Becque wrote with no other idea than to create living people, allowing them only so much of a plot as should be necessary to demonstrate their thoughts and consequent acts. For many years he unsuccessfully submitted his manuscripts to managers, but in the 'eighties his efforts brought forth fruit. Their intrinsic, apart from historical value, is clearly seen in the fact that both plays continue to draw large audiences at the Comédie Française and the Odéon.

Antoine is a bourgeois, a bourgeois of the solid, forceful, intelligent type of Brieux. With an almost brutal and dogged air of strength, he gives the impression of one who — endowed with a vision — will move mountains and override his subordinates without appearing to notice the result of his assiduity. Seated in his office at the Odéon one evening, I was at liberty to observe at close quarters his personal appearance. A tall man, with a marked stoop, his small blue eyes set wide apart, his large cheeks resting upon a stiff high collar, he spoke with gruff geniality, and straight to the point.

"The 'Théâtre Libre,' mon Dieu! It seems like ancient history! Well — here's all the material you want. I've kept the files — in there is a room full of letters! I may publish them some day, but, vous savez? it's the devil of a job! Take what you like.

"You asked me in your letter whether the choice of typical plays of the 'Théâtre Libre' you had made is a good one? Yes, Curel and Ancey and Jullien are representative, while Porto-Riche may serve to show something of the variety I attempted to make in our programs. Brieux, of course Brieux is 'Théâtre Libre,' but I understand he is already known in your country."

And briefly, but courteously, Antoine outlined his work, in somewhat the following manner. The main facts I have gleaned from stray articles and historical compilations, but I have tried to enter into the spirit of the subject from Antoine's point of view, and make what reservations I am forced to when that spirit seems in direct opposition to the truth.

André Antoine was born in 1858 at Limoges. He was sent to school at Paris at an early age, but was forced to go to work in an office at the age of thirteen. In 1877 he became an employee of the Gas Company at Paris, where he remained, with the exception of the years spent in military service, until his resignation, ten years later, when he founded his little theater. Antoine was always deeply interested in theatrical matters; as a child he attended classses in declamation and acting, and once aspired to enter the august Conservatoire, but failed to pass the preliminary examination. His vigorous natural acting, though lacking the polish necessary for entrance into the school of which he wished to become a member, never failed to impress the small audiences gathered together to witness the occasional amateur productions organized by the young enthusiast. From his little "Gymnase de la parole" he passed into the "Cercle Gaulois," another, slightly more ambitious, dramatic club. This club produced conventional plays, against which Antoine was soon to revolt. "Of what use" he said, "is it to give plays which can be seen anywhere?" Krauss, the director of the "Cercle," was unwilling to produce new works, so that Antoine was forced to secede and found what he called the "Théâtre Libre"— or Free Theater. In the tiny improvised playhouse in the Rue de l'Elysée des Beaux-Arts, on the "Butte de Montmartre," on the evening of March 30, 1887, took place the first production of the new society. "Mademoiselle Pomme" by Duranty and Paul Alexis; "Un Préfet," by Arthur Byl; "Jacques Damour," by Léon Hennique after Zola; and "La Cocarde," by Jules Vidal — two comedies and two "dramas," each in one act — these constituted the opening spectacle. With the exception of "Jacques Damour," the performance was a failure. All the heartrending mishaps incident to amateur performances seemed destined to occur on that fatal night. Had it not been for the profound impression created by the Hennique-Zola sketch, it is doubtful whether the Free Theater would have continued.

Antoine had spent all his salary, and something besides, to mount the first performance on March 30, but he determined to tempt Providence once more, and on the next convenient payday, just two months later, he presented two more plays: "La Nuit Bergamesque," a verse comedy by the poet Emile Bergerat, and a one-act "serious" play by Oscar Méténier, "En Famille." The first performance had attracted little attention, but that in May brought among others, Francisque Sarcey, Emile Zola, and Alphonse Daudet. "Contemporary dramatic art," says one enthusiastic historian, "was born that evening." But if that is a slight exaggeration, we may be assured that Antoine believed that it had, for he resigned from his position with the Gas Company in order to devote his entire time and energy to the direction of his theater. Sending out an appeal to many writers who thought they had original, unconventional plays, plays which no manager in Paris was willing to accept at the time, he received a great many manuscripts during the summer of 1887. That summer was occupied with many cares: a new theater — the "Gaité Montparnasse"— had to be fitted up, subscriptions to a series of performances taken, and no end of minor matters attended to. It is recorded that Antoine carried his subscription blanks to the homes of those who might be interested in the project, in order to save postage.

By October, Antoine had secured only thirty-five subscriptions. In order to escape the vigilance of the censor, his performances were made private:

individuals voluntarily subscribed and were "invited" to the theater. On October 12 was the first regular subscription performance of the Free Theater. "Soeur Philomène," a naturalistic play based upon the novel by the brothers de Goncourt, and "L'Evasion," a play in one act by Villiers de l'Isle Adam, made up that program. A month later Antoine introduced to his audience one of the typical Free Theater plays, "Esther Brandès," by Léon Hennique. On December 23, the "Genre Théâtre Libre" became permanently fixed in Jean Jullien's "La Sérénade."

By this time the Theater began to attract widespread attention, and before long it became a veritable storm-center of literary schools and sects. The progressives and reactionaries took sides aggressively, and battles waged. The result was a happy one for Antoine and his theater. He thrived on abuse and adverse criticism. Sarcey, the exponent of the "well-made" play and despot of the theatrical world, shrieked aloud that the new pieces were simply not plays — by which he meant that they were not plays of the Scribe-Sardou school. Which they were not.

Not content with introducing French plays alone, Antoine mounted Tolstoy's "The Power of Darkness" (February 10, 1888). This aroused a good deal of excitement.[1] The production of

[1] Before this play was produced, Antoine received a number of letters from dramatists and critics. Among these were protests from three masters of the stage of the day. Émile Augier says: "It is less a play than a novel in dialogue, the length of which would render it insupportable on our French stage." Dumas fils says: "From the point of view of our French stage, I do not think Tolstoy's play possible. It is too pessimistic;

this play was of incalculable benefit to the French stage: it demonstrated first that a so-called " undramatic " play could be made interesting and effective on the stage, and it paved the way for the production of the masterpieces of foreign contemporary drama in a country which is to this day only too ready to ignore foreign works on the ground that France still leads the world in the realm of the theater.

Antoine's productions of Tolstoy, Ibsen, Strindberg, and Björnson, have done much for the education of the modern French critic and theatergoer, coming at a time when the country was so far behind contemporary European dramatic literature.

The first season's significant contributions were " La Sérénade," of which further mention will be made later, and " The Power of Darkness." Yet a word should be said of Gustave Guiches and Henry Lavedan, whose " quarts d'heure," — light fragmentary scenes, satirical commentaries on society — opened the way for these two dramatists, and constituted a veritable theatrical début. Lavedan, later in " Le Nouveau jeu " and " Le Prince d'Aurec " did little more than enlarge upon his scenes and construct some sort of plot upon which they might be strung. Gustave Guiches, one of the most powerful of the less original dramatic writers of to-day, if he did not follow in the footsteps of his early collaborator, was at least

there is not a single sympathetic character . . ." Sardou says: " It is cruelly beautiful and essentially true, but it is written to be read and not seen. In my opinion it is not playable. Everything that can be done to make it possible for the stage will result only in spoiling it. . . ."

encouraged to write plays, which have been seen on the best stages in Paris.

The end of the first subscription year found Antoine poor in pocket, but correspondingly rich in experience; the seven productions — in which seventeen plays figured — had exhausted his small capital, and again the indefatigable producer faced a financial problem. Yet before the question became very serious he found that the number of subscribers had become so great that he had to find a larger theater in order to accommodate them. He then engaged the "Théâtre des Menus-Plaisirs," remodeled it, and started his second season. By this time the little band of amateurs, under the dictatorial head of Antoine, had come to be recognized as a highly efficient company of original actors. The plays, owing to their subject-matter and unconventional treatment of new themes, had attracted so much attention that even old and hardened theater-goers flocked to the Menus-Plaisirs, if only to scoff.

Late in the year 1888 Georges de Porto-Riche, known previously to that time as the author of a few slight volumes of poems and four or five not very successful poetic dramas, saw his "Chance de Françoise" produced by the Free Theater. The immediate success of this delicate little comedy doubtless encouraged its author to write his greatest play, "Amoureuse," which saw the stage not long after. Another important play of the second season was Léon Hennique's noble historical tragedy, "La Mort du Duc d'Enghien." Neither of these plays was what is known as the "genre

Théâtre Libre "— as Jullien's "La Sérénade" was — nor was Catulle Mendès' "La Reine Fiammette," which was in verse. These plays, together with the Goncourts' "La Patrie en danger," serve further to illustrate that Antoine was not trying to destroy the old so much as to make way for the new, and at the same time, accept so much of the old as was sincere and beautiful. However, Zola, with "Madeleine" continued the tradition of the Naturalists. Georges Ancey, the author of "La Dupe," was trying his wings with a three-act comedy, "Les Inséparables."

The seasons from 1888 to 1893 inclusive marked the period of greatest activity and contributed the largest number of good plays of the entire Antoine movement. About ninety plays were produced, most of them new French works, although Hauptmann, Ibsen, Turgenev, Björnson, Strindberg, and Tolstoy were represented by some of their best works.

The season of 1889–90 was one of the most fruitful and historically important of the series: Ibsen's "Ghosts," Brieux's "Ménages d'artistes," and Jean Aicard's "Le Père Lebonnard" were all seen for the first time in France. Brieux certainly owes a great deal to Antoine. When he was editing a small newspaper in Rouen he sent the manuscript of his first play of distinct merit to the new theater. Antoine accepted and played "Ménages d'artistes" and encouraged the young author to send further plays. The next was "Blanchette," one of the finest achievements of its gifted and vigorous author. It is doubtful whether Brieux would have continued to write his second play had it not been for Antoine's encouragement. In his dedication of "Blanchette" Brieux says: "My Dear Friend, For ten years I peddled my plays to every manager in Paris; more often than not, they were not even read. Thanks to you, thanks to the 'Théâtre Libre,' I am at last able to learn my business as a dramatist, and now here is the second of my plays which you have produced. I wish to thank you in public."

Jean Aicard, poet of the South, though not primarily a dramatist, has written at least one play of superlative merit: "Le Père Lebonnard" has been seen, since it was first produced by Antoine, in nearly every theatrical center of the world, and still remains in the repertory of the Comédie Française and in that of the great Italian actor, Ermete Novelli.

Pierre Wolff, one of the best-known dramatists of to-day, was another whose plays were first accepted and produced at the Free Theater. In France, "Le Secret de Polichinelle" and "Le Ruisseau" are considered among the best and most charming works of the day. In the United States Madame Nazimova played in M. Wolff's recent comedy, "Les Marionettes."

Georges Courteline, Paul Ginisty, François de Curel, Albert Guinon, and Romain Coolus, unknown in the early 'nineties, all débutants at the Free Theater, have since achieved distinct success. Of these, Curel is by all odds the most significant. There is little doubt that such writers as Courteline and Coolus, and perhaps Guinon and Ginisty, would have attained the rank of "successful" dramatists, but had it not been for the foresight and determined energy of Antoine, Curel would probably have never had a hearing. Antoine literally forced a hearing for the earlier works of this writer.

The pioneer work of the Free Theater was soon accomplished: in 1887 a small revolutionary protest led by a comparatively obscure amateur, by 1894, it had begun to decline. So well had Antoine combatted the conventions he had set himself to destroy, that seven years after the attack his enemies had for the most part become friends or at least distant admirers and sympathizers, or else imitators. Many reasons have been suggested to account for the decadence of the Theater: commercialism, tours, lack of good actors for want of funds, poor choice of plays — but the fact is that the public had become accustomed to the novelty of the ideas set forth by the new movement: every one became in a sense revolutionary, so that there was nothing to revolt against.

The commercial theaters, seeing that the plays of the Free Theater dramatists were valuable, at once received Brieux, Wolff, Curel, Porto-Riche, and Courteline, with open arms. The actors, trained by Antoine, could not be kept together on the small salaries which were the natural result of the very limited number of productions — two only of each new play. They went forth and without difficulty obtained lucrative positions in many of the best theaters in Paris.

Realizing that his work was over, Antoine resigned in 1896, leaving his theater — re-named the "Théâtre Antoine" — in the hands of Larochelle, and became an actor. But in 1906 he accepted the directorship of the Odéon. For over seven years he struggled against insufficient subsidies, and now has to his credit a large number of new productions, besides some of the worthiest of classical revivals as director of this government theater. As this book is about to go to press, the news comes from Paris that Antoine, worn out with his gigantic task and ruined financially, has resigned.[2]

Among the numerous followers of Antoine, Lugné-Poë and his "Théâtre de l'Oeuvre" should first be mentioned. This society is one of the most important in the world. For over twenty years the indefatigable "Lugné" has made it a point to introduce new and original French plays as well as foreign works. These he has produced in Paris for short runs, but his greatest contribution to the art of the theater has been his long and extended tours: in Africa, England, South America, Russia, Belgium, Germany, Servia —

[2] In a letter to the *Figaro,* dated April 8, 1914, he writes to the Minister of Public Instruction and Fine Arts: "M. le Ministre: I regret that I have to ask you to accept my resignation. The various solutions we discussed during the meeting yesterday have not by this morning come to pass. It was unavoidable that I should be unable to cope with these overwhelming financial obligations. At this juncture I see no other course open to me but the one I am pursuing. I leave the Odéon with many regrets in spite of the seven abominable years I have spent there. In spite of your kind assistance during these past few days the production of 'Psyché' [Molière's] last night cost me much more than the figure of the receipts. I must therefore courageously face the prospect of giving up my dream of a prosperous art-theater, and apply myself energetically to solving a terrible problem wherein I shall lose my honor as a business man and the decoration so kindly given me by the liberality of the Government. Yours, etc., André Antoine."

nearly every country except the United States. Lugné-Poë it was who first introduced Maeterlinck to the French, and the world at large; he has likewise mounted hundreds of plays, among them the most typical works of the German, Russian, and Scandinavian schools. Of late, his special matinées in Paris have afforded the somewhat blasé audiences of that city the opportunity of becoming acquainted with Synge. The " Playboy of the Western World," given in the " Théâtre Antoine " by the " Théâtre de l'Oeuvre " in December 1913, served at least to open the eyes of the French to the fact that there was a drama in Ireland, even if the production left much to be desired. Lugné-Poë determined to show his people that France was not the only country in the world which was important theatrically, has continued fearlessly and intelligently to force his compatriots to recognize the value of the foreigners.

A word may be said at this point of a few other similar ventures. The first, the " Cercle des Escholiers," founded at the same time as the Free Theater, is a private association, founded by and now under the leadership of M. Georges Bourdon — of the " Figaro "— to whom I am indebted for a good deal of information on his own theater as well as on the Antoine venture. The " Théâtre d'Art," Carré's " Matinées du jeudi," Jacques Rouché's " Théâtre des Arts," and Jacques Copeau's " Théâtre du Vieux-colombier," founded about a year ago, may all be traced to the influence of the Free Theater.

THE THEORY OF THE FREE THEATER

Antoine founded his Free Theater with the idea of inducing new and original dramatists to present works which the prejudice of managers and public otherwise kept from the stage. The French stage of the day was so conventional that only plays written according to accepted standards would attract audiences. At least, this is what the managers thought — and the result was the same. Together with conventional plays went conventional acting and conventional stage-setting.

Antoine felt that all this was wrong, and he set it right. Adolphe Thalasso briefly sums up the "esthétique" of the new theater in his "Le Théâtre Libre" (Mercure de France, 1909): "Plays in which life supplies movement begin to take the place of those in which movement supplied life. Complicated plots give way to simple stories; the play of intrigue is offset by the study of reality; characters become natural, classic; the tragic and comic are no longer mingled; the genres have become distinct. Interminable, vagarious plays give way to short, concise, rapid ones. The tirade disappears; bombast and bathos are relegated to the background . . . no more 'raisonneurs' . . . facts alone explain the philosophy of the piece. The eternally sympathetic and benevolent character is likewise driven out. The authors go to the very sources of life for the morality of their plays. So much the worse for morality if their 'moral' is immoral! Such is life — and the theater should be not an amusement, but an image of life. Technical gymnastics are thrown aside: the human heart needs more than tricks of the trade in order to be explained. . . . The theater of to-day must be a revolt against that of yesterday. As in all revolutions, there is a good deal of exaggeration, for the new methods are driven home with hammering blows. To attain the desired end, the revolutionists overstep the limit, and in striking down the guilty, the innocent are not spared."

This at least is a fairly accurate statement of the theory of the Free Theater, but the theory, it goes without saying, was not always lived up to. Scribe and Sardou were too deeply imbedded in the consciousness of the French nation to allow a few reformers to escape their influence. The long speeches, tirades, asides, and soliloquies which the innovators scorned — in theory — are often to be found in the earlier plays of Jullien, Curel, Ancey, and Brieux. Yet those finer qualities — a love of truth in the analysis of character, a desire to get nearer to the life and motives of the average human being which were encouraged by Antoine, — were, in spite of occasional slips and back-slidings, early manifested, and to this day have borne rich fruit.

THE ACTING

The Free Theater evolved a style of acting all its own. That style may be called Naturalistic. Its greatest contribution was largely a negative one. It constituted a protest against the Conservatoire, where the art of acting was handed down by tradition from one famous actor to the next. There was one way of acting Harpagon, or Tartufe, or Phèdre, and only one way; the students at the Conservatoire received their instruction from pupils of Samson or Got or Talma, who in turn had received them from the great actors of their generation. The process tended to eliminate originality, although it produced an average of finished work which in the French classics is at least admissible. But with the advent of a new school of drama, a new school of acting was indispensable.

When Antoine dared to turn his back to the audience, the audience jeered. To-day there is scarcely an actor in Paris who has not learned from Antoine. Antoine knew what he was about, and so well did he insinuate his new ideas into the company, that before long his actors left him and entered the large commercial theaters on the boulevards. Nearly every theater in Paris, including the Comédie Française and the Odéon, either has at present or has had within the past few years, at least one former Free Theater actor in its staff of players.

THE DRAMATISTS

The mere enumeration of dramatic writers whose first works (or first save one) were heard at the Free Theater would fill four pages. Of those dramatists who are to-day either in the front rank of accepted playwrights may be mentioned: Brieux, Curel, Coolus, Courteline, Marcel Prévost, Lucien Descaves, Lavedan, Porto-Riche, Gustave Guiches, André Picard, Pierre Wolff, Emile Fabre, Paul Ginisty, Armand Ephraim, and Jean Aicard. Among those who are no longer writing, but who largely contributed to the founding of the movement and standardizing of the new methods, are: Jean Jullien, Georges Ancey, Paul Alexis, Emile Zola, Gaston Salandri, Henry Céard, Léon Hennique, the Goncourts, and Villiers de l'Isle Adam.

Brieux.— Eugène Brieux (born 1858 at Paris) is a true son of the Free Theater. His first important play, "Ménages d'Artistes" was fairly successful, and the encouragement received from this first production was largely instrumental in starting his theatrical career. "Blanchette" (1892) [3] was one of the greatest successes of the day, and is now frequently revived at the Comédie Française and in the provinces. Brieux's vigorous and straightforward manner of attacking the social abuses of his time was in all likelihood fostered by the freedom from restraint which was the chief glory of the Free Theater. That "Damaged Goods" and "The Red Robe" and "The Three Daughters of M. Dupont" have been accepted by the theater-going publics of the most important nations of the world is to some extent due to Antoine.

François de Curel.—Viscount François de Curel (born 1854 at Metz) is without doubt the most original and clear-minded dramatist of recent times. His comparatively few plays deal almost exclusively with abnormal human characteristics; were they not treated from the psychological viewpoint and written in a literary though thoroughly dramatic style they would be termed melodramas. "L'Envers d'une Sainte," his first play, is an

[3] "Blanchette" would have been included in the present volume had it not already appeared in the Fall of 1913: "Blanchette and the Escape" (Luce).

extraordinary and noble study of a woman's conscience; it is a distinct contribution to criminal psychology. "Le Repas du Lion" is another study in the gradual metamorphosis of a conscience. His latest play (winter 1914) "La Danse devant le Miroir" is one of the most daring and searching analyses of the mind and heart of a young girl in the realm of French drama; beside it, Henri Bataille's "La Vierge folle" is pale and unconvincing. A slow worker, holding himself aloof from society, from the world of the practical theater, caring little for the conventions of the stage, Curel is not a popular idol. He is respected by the many, warmly appreciated by the few.

"Les Fossiles" was presented in its original form at the Free Theater in 1892. The play was badly cast so that the performance was a failure, but in 1900, after some revision, it was given a fair hearing at the Comédie Française, and achieved considerable success. "Les Fossiles" comes the nearest of any of its author's plays to the popular conception of what a play should be. There is more action and less abstract psychology in it than in any other Curel work, yet the basic idea is never for a moment sacrificed for theatrical effects. Curel, an aristocrat himself, is enough of an artist to adopt a transcendental point of view and comment upon the nobility of the time. "Les Fossiles" is the story of a noble family which gives up life, happiness and even individual honor in order to save the family name. The aspirations, struggles, above all, that undying, deep-rooted desire to live in the future are pictured in this play with unforgettable vividness. Besides being a comment on and a picture of life, the play contains an ideal: Robert de Chantemelle in his will and in his life, attempts to direct the energies of his family from becoming fossilized to the nobler realization of their duties to society and the State. If the play contains a lesson at all it is that.

Jean Jullien.—Jean Jullien (born at Lyon, 1854) fixed the style of the Free Theater play once for all in "La Sérénade." His plays, and more especially his theories [4] — that "a play is a slice of life presented artistically on the stage" is his best-known — became at once a sort of confession of faith for the Theater. "La Sérénade" (1887) stands for the younger generation, which stood for the presentation in all its ugliness of the "other side" of life. Its brutality, its exaggeration, its sordidness, are not so much signs of a positive philosophy of life, as a savage revolt against the lay-figures of the conventional drama of the nineteenth century; Mme. Cottin would surely not have been painted so black were the Little Nell heroines of Augier and Scribe and Sardou not quite so dazzlingly virginal.

Jullien, in this play as well as in his other important play, "Le Maître," was too conscientious, too unbending and uncompromising, to meet the popular demand in theatrical goods, so that with the close of the Free Theater his activity practically ceased.

Georges Ancey.— Georges Ancey (born 1860 at Paris) like Jullien, was too independent to secure and hold public favor. Yet his power of ob-

[4] See "Le Théatre vivant" (Charpentier, Paris, 1892).

servation, his mordant satire, his trenchant and occasionally overdrawn pictures of middle-class family life, formed one of the greatest contributions to the movement. "Les Inséparables" (1889) and "L'Ecole des Veufs" (1889) are splendid examples of Ancey's comic power, while "La Dupe" (1891) presents him in the light of a commentator on the darker side of human nature. The play suffers from exaggeration of character which at times seems all but puerile, but the true tragedy of the situation, the inherent power and irony of the story, the numerous striking scenes, more than counterbalance the somewhat amateurish shortcomings.

Georges de Porto-Riche.—Georges de Porto-Riche (born at Bordeaux, 1849) while he did not greatly aid the new movement, received help and inspiration from it. His first success, "La Chance de Françoise" (1888) must surely have paved the way for his masterpiece, "Amoureuse" (1891), a play which has exercised as great an influence upon the contemporary French drama as any other of the late nineteenth century. Henry Bataille and Maurice Donnay owe much to Porto-Riche.

Antoine's acceptance of "La Chance de Françoise" was but another indication of his breadth of view. He did not insist on sordid middle-class dramas: his idea was to produce what seemed good and original. Porto-Riche had a charming character study, Antoine liked it, and produced it. His good judgment has by half a dozen revivals at the best-known theaters of the capital been amply justified.

THE INFLUENCE OF THE FREE THEATER

The influence of Antoine's ideas on managers was great and wide-spread. These were led to inquire into the validity of the traditions they had for so long blindly accepted, and cast aside what was superfluous. A new generation of actors arose which though it owed a good deal to its own intelligence and initiative was yet decidedly influenced by Antoine. The vigorous acting of Lucien Guitry, the exquisite and delicate art of Madame Simone — to mention no others — seem but the natural development from the little group of amateurs which gathered together in 1887 in the Rue de l'Elysée des Beaux-Arts.

" I believe," says Curel, " that the greatest service rendered by the Free Theater was that of liberating the modern French stage of all schools and literary coteries. A day will come when greater justice will be done our dramatic era, when the full extent of its originality and independence will be fully realized. The originality and independence of which I speak are due for the most part to the Free Theater."

If the Free Theater has exercised the greatest influence over the modern French stage, which it has, we must not be too hasty to conclude that the entire modern movement was due to Antoine. It so happened that he came at the right time, that the " dramatic crisis " would sooner or later have precipitated some sort of revolution. Antoine helped crystallize the ideas that were in the air. He was far from a perfect manager, nor was his judgment unerring. He was human enough, at one time, to desire to leave the theater he had founded, and become a salaried actor; at another, he nearly ruined his theater by selecting plays which were accommodated to the actors with little reference to the merit of the piece. His productions at the Odéon (granted even that he was working at a terrible disadvantage) were often slipshod, unworthy even of those "commercial" theaters he had so often ridiculed and whose conventional methods he had spent the greater part of his life in destroying. If he has done valuable work, he has done harm; if he freed the stage from one set of conventions he has gone a long way to impose another set, which may in time be as injurious as those he destroyed. Yet that is only what might have been expected of a man who was — permit the platitude — no more than human. Antoine's work belonged to a particular period, and that period was the turning-point in the history of the modern French theater. While he was forced to fight his way his work was sincere and for the most part beneficial. If to-day other nations — like Germany and Russia — have gone beyond him, and if certain managers in his own land have taken what was best from his work, he is not to be blamed. For about ten years he was the best and most influential producer in Europe, and a revolutionary to whom the highest tribute should be paid.

Antoine was the prophet of the transition: Naturalism in fiction was bound to bring forth Naturalism in the theater. Naturalism was a passing phase: we have seen its rise and fall. If Antoine helped Naturalism in the theater to rise and fall, he has honestly done his share — a generous share — in the evolution of an art which is advancing, although we are as yet unable to determine toward just what end.

To MM. Brieux, Curel, and Antoine I owe my deepest gratitude for a great deal of valuable information on the movement in which they played so important a part. In numerous conversations these gentlemen have been unsparing in time and trouble, and afforded me an insight into their work which I could not otherwise have enjoyed.

Barrett H. Clark.

ALPHABETICAL LIST OF PLAYS PRODUCED AT THE FREE THEATER YEARS 1887–1896, INCLUSIVE [1]

A bas le progrès. Edmond de Goncourt.
L'Abbé Pierre. Marcel Prévost.
L'Affranchie. Maurice Biollay.
Ahasuère. Hermann Heijermans.
L'Amant de sa femme. Aurélien Scholl.
L'Amant du Christ. Rodolphe Darzens.
Amants éternels. André Corneau et H. Gerbault.
L'Ame invisible. Claude Berton.
L'Ancien. Léon Cladel.
L'Argent. Emile Fabre.
L'Assomption de Hannele Mattern. Gerhart Hauptmann.
Au temps de la Ballade. Georges Bois.
Le Baiser. Théodore de Banville.
La Belle au bois rêvant. Fernand Mazade.
La Belle Opération. Julien Sermet.
Belle Petite. André Corneau.
Blanchette. Brieux.
Boubouroche. Georges Courteline.
Les Bouchers. Fernand Icres.
Le Canard Sauvage. Ibsen.
La Casserole. Oscar Méténier.
La Chance de Françoise. Georges de Porto-Riche.

[1] From "Le Théâtre Libre" by Adolphe Thalasso (Mercure de France, 1909).

Les Chapons. Lucien Descaves et Georges Darien.
La Chevalerie Rustique. Giovanni Verga.
La Cocarde. Jules Vidal.
Le Coeur révélateur. Ernest Laumann.
Cœurs simples. Sutter-Laumann.
Le Comte Witold. Stanislas Rzewuski.
Conte de Noël. Auguste Linert.
Le Cor fleuri. Mikhael Ephraim.
Le Cuivre. Paul Adam et André Picard.
Dans le Guignol. Jean Aicard.
Dans le Rêve. Louis Mullem.
Deux Tourtereaux. Paul Ginisty et Jules Guérin.
Le Devoir. Louis Bruyerre.
Dialogue inconnu. Alfred de Vigny.
La Dupe. Georges Ancey.
L'Echéance. Jean Jullien.
L'Ecole des Veufs. Georges Ancey.
Elen. Villiers de l'Isle Adam.
En Détresse. Henry Fèvre.
En Famille. Oscar Méténier.
En l'attendant. Léon Roux
L'Envers d'une Sainte. François de Curel.
Esther Brandès. Léon Hennique.
L'Etoile Rouge. Henry Fèvre.
L'Evasion. Villiers de l'Isle Adam.
La Femme de Tabarin. Catulle Mendès.
Les Fenêtres. Jules Perrin et Claude Couturier.
La Fille d'Artaban. Alfred Mortier.
La Fille Elisa. Jean Ajalbert.
La Fin de Lucie Pellegrin. Paul Alexis.
La Fin du vieux temps. Paul Anthelm.

Les Fossiles. François de Curel.
Les Fourches caudines. Maurice Le Corbeiller.
Les Frères Zemganno. Paul Alexis et Oscar Méténier.
La Fumée puis la flamme. Joseph Caragull.
Grand-papa. Claude Berton.
La Grappin. Gaston Salandri.
L'Honneur. Henry Fèvre.
Inceste d'âmes. Jean Laurenty et Fernand Hauser.
L'Inquiétude. Jules Perrin et Claude Courturier.
Les Inséparables. Georges Ancey.
Jacques Bouchard. Pierre Wolff.
Jacques Damour. Léon Hennique.
Jeune Premier. Paul Ginisty.
Leurs filles. Pierre Wolff.
Lidoire. Georges Courteline.
Madeleine. Emile Zola.
Mademoiselle Fifi. Oscar Méténier.
Mademoiselle Julie. August Strindberg.
Mademoiselle Pomme. Paul Alexis et Duranty.
Le Maître. Jean Jullien.
Mariage d'argent. Eugène Bourgeois.
Les Maris de leurs filles. Pierre Wolff.
Matapan. Emile Moreau.
Mélie. Georges Docquois.
Le Ménage Brésile. Romain Coolus.
Ménages d'artistes. Brieux.
La Meule. Georges Lecomte.
Mirages. Georges Lecomte.
Le Missionaire. Marcel Luguet.
Monsieur Bute. Maurice Biollay.

Simone. Louis de Gramont.
Soeur Philomène. Arthur Byl et Jules Vidal.
Soldat et mineur. Jean Malafayde.
Son petit coeur. Louis Marsollau.
La Tante Léontine. Maurice Boniface et Edouard Bodin.
Les Tisserands. Gerhart Hauptmann.
Tout pour l'honneur. Henry Céard.
Un beau soir. Maurice Vaucaire.
Une Faillite. Björnstjerne Björnson.
Une Journée parlementaire. Maurice Barrès.
Une nouvelle école. Louis Mullem.
Un préfet. Arthur Byl.
Valet de Coeur. Maurice Vaucaire.

REFERENCES

Among the great mass of contemporary criticism, collected from periodicals, may be mentioned: Sarcey, *Quarante ans de Théâtre;* Jules Lemaître, *Impressions de Théâtre;* Emile Faguet, *Propos de Théâtre;* and Edmond Stoullig, *Les Annales du Théâtre et de la Musique.*

Books and essays on the Free Theater: Adolphe Thalasso, "Le Théâtre Libre" (Mercure de France); Augustin Filon, "De Dumas à Rostand" (Colin); Jean Jullien, "Le Théâtre Vivant" (Charpentier); "Le Théâtre Libre" (privately printed brochure, Mai 1890).

Individual biographies of Brieux, Curel, Porto-Riche, Courteline, Lucien Descaves, and Jean Aicard, in the *Célébrités d'Aujourd'hui* series (Sansot).

Further bibliographical and biographical material in: George Moore, "Impressions and Opinions" (Brentano); Barrett H. Clark, *The Continental Drama of To-day* (Holt). Magazines: *The Drama,* Nos. 2 and 11.

The Fossils

(*Les Fossiles*)

A Play in Four Acts

By

FRANCOIS DE CUREL

AUTHORIZED TRANSLATION BY

BARRETT H. CLARK

Produced for the first time in its original form, at Paris in the Théâtre Libre, November 29, 1892; revived, in its present form, by the company of the Théâtre Français, in the Odéon Theater, May 21, 1900.

PERSONS REPRESENTED:

THE DUKE OF CHANTEMELLE
ROBERT DE CHANTEMELLE
NICOLAS
A FARMER
A COUNTRY NEIGHBOR
A SERVANT
THE DUCHESS DE CHANTEMELLE
CLAIRE DE CHANTEMELLE
HÉLÈNE VATRIN
A NUN

CASTS:

	1892
THE DUKE DE CHANTEMELLE	MM. Antoine
ROBERT DE CHANTEMELLE	Camis
NICOLAS	Arquillière
A FARMER	Pens-Arlès
A COUNTRY NEIGHBOR	Gémier
A SERVANT	Verse
THE DUCHESS DE CHANTEMELLE	Mmes. Besnier
CLAIRE DE CHANTEMELLE	Berthe Bady
HÉLÈNE VATRIN	Jeanne Dulac
A NUN	Méréane

	1900
THE DUKE DE CHANTEMELLE	MM. Paul Mounet
ROBERT DE CHANTEMELLE	Le Bargy
NICOLAS	Laugier
A FARMER	Ravet
A COUNTRY NEIGHBOR.	Joliet
A SERVANT	Laty
THE DUCHESS DE CHANTEMELLE	Mmes. Pierson
CLAIRE DE CHANTEMELLE	Bartet
HÉLÈNE VATRIN	Wanda de Bencza
A NUN	Delvair

THE FOSSILS

ACT I

[*A large country house in the Ardennes.— A spacious wainscotted room; to the right, windows partially concealed by thick curtains; to the left, a high fireplace between two doors. At the back, a large doorway opening into a vestibule. The paneling around this door, as well as the walls of the room, is covered with panoplies, hunting trophies, old armor, genealogical charts, and maps of ancient domains. The furnishings are severe; the room breathes an air of feudalism.*

It is evening; a single lamp gives out a sickly light into the room. From time to time the fire, which is concealed for the most part in ashes, shoots forth little flames. Outside, a storm is beginning; the whistling of the wind is heard.

Enter Claire. She looks quickly about her, goes to the window and raises the curtain to look into the night, but the inside shutters are closed. She makes a little gesture of impatience, then goes at once to the door at the back, and is about to leave the room when a servant enters carrying an armful of wood. She intercepts him and asks]

CLAIRE. There is a carriage outside from town; whose is it?

SERVANT. The doctor's, Mademoiselle.

CLAIRE. The doctor from Paris?

SERVANT. The doctor from Paris and the one from town also.

CLAIRE. But the consultation was not to take place until to-morrow?

SERVANT. I heard the gentlemen telling Madame la duchesse that the doctor from Paris has to make a speech to-morrow before the Academy of Science. So he telegraphed and said he would come to-day. The telegram didn't arrive because of the frost that broke all the wires this side of Sedan.

CLAIRE. Do you know whether the doctors are to take dinner here?

SERVANT. Oh, no, Mademoiselle; they didn't even unhitch their horses. When I was coming up-stairs just now, I overheard them talking with Madame la duchesse; they're probably gone by this time.

CLAIRE. Has my father come in yet?

SERVANT. I haven't seen any one.

CLAIRE. Very well!

[*She sits beside a table, down-stage, and leans upon it, meditating. The servant puts the wood by the fireplace, lays a log on the fire, and goes out. After a moment, Claire rises, opens the door at the back, listens, then comes back to the fireplace, standing before it, her head resting upon the stone mantel.*

Enter the Duchess at the back. Her expression is one of great sadness; her eyes are red from crying. Claire turns round, and the Duchess throws herself precipitately into her arms.]

DUCHESS. Your poor brother!

CLAIRE. Worse?!

DUCHESS. Yes! We have to send him south. He will never come back to us — I know it!

CLAIRE. Is it that bad?

DUCHESS. The doctors gave him all sorts of encouragement. I don't know whether he belived them, but I knew well enough they weren't telling the truth! I saw them to their carriage, and the moment they were saying Good-by — I was on the steps, with snow on my feet, and I was quite sure Robert was out of hearing,— I asked them for the truth.

CLAIRE. But if they're sending him south —?

DUCHESS. He will never recover! Perhaps the climate at Nice will prolong his life for a few months — perhaps! [*Holding back her tears.*] Here, they told me, it was only a question of days —

[*She falls into a chair, her face buried in a handkerchief. Claire, standing as before at the fireplace, is crying also, but she controls her feelings.*]

CLAIRE. They must be exaggerating!

DUCHESS. Our only hope is in God! — [*After a pause.*] What a blow for your father!

CLAIRE [*dryly*]. Yes, it is! But he will be able to survive: hasn't he his hunting, his dogs, his horses, and all that?

DUCHESS [*with severity*]. Claire, you never miss an opportunity of saying something disagreeable about your father; why? You didn't use to do that; I remember when you adored him. Why have you changed so suddenly? What —?

CLAIRE [*embarrassed*]. I haven't changed — perhaps I'm not so sympathetic and open as when I was a young girl — that's all. You may be sure I feel keenly for him.

DUCHESS. It will be terrible. His dogs and horses will be of little use to him now. He loves Robert, and then — he might perhaps have had some consolation —! If Robert had only had a brother, if he weren't the only son; if our name, the title of Duke, weren't about to die out — do you understand?

CLAIRE. Do I understand? [*Tense with excitement.*] The Dukes of Chantemelle! Their names are on every page of the history of France! It's terrible to have Robert so near the end,— to think that after his death all our glory, our almost royal greatness, will be only a dream of the past! If I am only a woman, I am proud of the name of Chantemelle! As proud as Father! Oh, what he will suffer when he comes in and hears the news! — Listen, Mother, I always intended never to get married, so that my share of the family fortune would go to Robert: a Duke de Chantemelle must live up to his name! —

DUCHESS. You are a true daughter of your father — and Robert is like you, too: you live in the past, it claims you, but you never realize how much the present forgets you — Times have changed! — Let the Duke de Chantemelle cease to exist, and the world will feel no loss. [*Sobbing.*] Only I, with my mother's heart—!

[*Robert enters, overhearing the last few words, a witness of the distress of his mother and sister. He is a man of distinguished bearing, with a pale face, feverish eyes, hollow cheeks, and flat chest. He gives the impression of one who is fighting bravely against disease and death.*]

ROBERT. Courage, Mother! [*Smiling sadly.*] I'm still alive!

DUCHESS [*rising in alarm*]. My child! You are not in the slightest danger! That is, the doctors said nothing definite! You know what they told you: a winter in Nice will give you new life!

ROBERT. That's what *you* said, Mother: they said that a winter in Nice would do me a great deal of good, that was all! It's something, of course! [*Ironically.*] Well, let us believe them—

DUCHESS. Of course, we must believe them! They impressed it on me again just as they were leaving.

ROBERT [*impatiently*]. Oh, very well! Has Father come in yet?

CLAIRE. No. The snow is so deep! It's so cold!

ROBERT [*with a sigh*]. I can imagine what's happened! They must have shot a number of boars; in this weather, it would be easy. Probably they wounded a big one, and chased him along his bloody trail until dark, for leagues and leagues! I can see them now, tired out, dragging one foot after the other — and the wounded dogs, and the hunters with icicles in their beards. [*Sighing again.*] And just one year ago I was doing all that!

CLAIRE [*with a forced smile*]. Do you regret it, slipping over the icy places, with a dog howling at your heels?

ROBERT. Yes, I regret the times when we galloped over the wide fields, Claire, you and I, and jumped the ditches and hedges — Now here I am, a horseman good for nothing, who sees his companion dashing away at full gallop over and beyond the horizon — while I —

CLAIRE [*holding back the tears*]. His companion — doesn't ride like that, any more,— without him! [*Overcome by her tears, quickly.*] If they didn't have good luck to-day Father's coming home in an awful humor. I'll have a good fire built in his bed-room. [*She goes out immediately.*]

ROBERT [*going to the Duchess, who is trying to assume an untroubled expression. He takes her hands, forces her to look into his face and, after a short silence*]. Now that we're alone, Mother, no more ceremonies! I haven't any illusions left about my condition; and you, you don't hope —!

DUCHESS. But I tell you —

ROBERT. Treat me like a man: I should be the first Chantemelle to shrink before death! — I once hoped for a different end, but this is only a better occasion to show courage, moral courage: not the kind that wins battles!

DUCHESS [*in an undertone*]. You talk so

cold-bloodedly! Your giving in to a Power against which no resistance is permitted is fearful! There are some times when that Power which we ought to bless even when it strikes us — [*Breaking out into sobs.*] Oh, I can't bear it! I can't bear it!

ROBERT. My giving in is not so hard as you think: I had foreseen the blow, I've been preparing for it during the past few weeks. My mind is quite at ease —

DUCHESS [*with an outburst of feeling*]. Then if you had to — leave us, you would regret nothing? Your father? Your mother? Your sister? No one, nothing? [*She sobs.*]

ROBERT. I shall have terrible regrets! I can hardly speak of them, when I think how much energy I need. It would be a great deal easier to brave out the whole thing!

[*He throws himself into a chair, exhausted, and hides his face in his hands.*]

DUCHESS. Poor child!

ROBERT [*raises his head and speaks to himself*]. If I'm sick, I've got to come to that! — Mother, I have a very serious matter to talk to you about — the happiness of my last days depends on it. I want you to promise me something.

DUCHESS [*rising*]. What is it?

ROBERT. It's about Mademoiselle Vatrin —

DUCHESS [*dryly*]. I can't imagine what you have to say about her. If it were about any one else — She is a young woman without a sou, whom I took care of because her mother was at boarding-school with me. The girl owes everything she has to me, and I have even promised her a small dowry! Until she finds a husband, I am allowing her to associate with your sister: Claire broods so much during the year I thought it wise to let her have a friend of her own age. See how grateful she is!

ROBERT [*seated, his head bent over his knees, his eyes fixed on the floor*]. Mademoiselle Vatrin is incapable of ingratitude. You must have had some good reason for getting her out of the way that summer! I doubt whether she has forgotten your kindness.

DUCHESS. You doubt?—I should think I did have good reasons for doing what I did! Mademoiselle Vatrin was much too familiar with you men, much too familiar for a young woman of twenty-five! I let her know she was overstepping the limits! Then she left.

ROBERT. She told me about it, and also that you offered her a pension, which she refused.

DUCHESS. Did she tell you that? You?! By what right? Why—?

ROBERT [*rising*]. Yes, she was my mistress. We loved one another deeply. What you called her familiarity was merely what we failed to have the presence of mind to hide. That was why you didn't understand.

DUCHESS [*deeply and strangely troubled, as she takes his hands in hers*]. Robert, you cannot imagine, you will never know what I feel now, when you tell me this!

ROBERT. You suppose, do you, that I am going to beg you to let me marry her? No.

Hélène knows what tremendous opposition she would meet with from the family.

DUCHESS. Marry her? I never thought of it. Why —! I was so sad this evening, and now I am so different. We should never lose hope —

ROBERT. Your love for me, Mother, is wonderful! My love for that girl fills you with happiness. Don't deny it, I see it in your face! It is as if you considered that my love for her formed a strong bond between me and — life! Well, if you're not too angry, I'm happy!

DUCHESS [*beaming*]. I am angry, and I blame you very much. How can I keep from blaming you for your irregular conduct — think of it, she was one of Claire's own friends! Your sister might have suspected! It was an insult to her! I don't want to scold you any more, Robert, your life is so sad! I'm only too glad to see you smile sometimes!

ROBERT [*smiling*]. I know very well you are not quite unforgiving. If you will be absolutely frank for a single second, I'll show you that you are very well satisfied with me.

DUCHESS. Satisfied that you seduced a young woman under my very roof, a woman who was under my protection! A friend of your own sister Claire?!

ROBERT. You can find many excellent reasons to prove that I have done wrong, but there is another matter — which is anything but unfortunate — something that you are always thinking about.

DUCHESS [*smiling*]. *All* the time?

ROBERT. Well, yes! There, you're beaming! Tell me now, why are you so glad?

DUCHESS. Why —?

ROBERT. Yes, why?

DUCHESS [*deciding to make some sort of answer*]. It might do some good — [*After a pause.*] Have you ever noticed? I was very unhappy — at one time, I thought there was something between your father and Mademoiselle Vatrin — I was so jealous and humiliated —!

ROBERT. Mother! It was I all the time! Oh, I was so happy! My happiness overflowed! When a river overflows its banks, who can see its usual course? — You were very tender just now — and you had no idea why!

DUCHESS. But I wasn't alone in my suspicions: I am almost positive that Claire was haunted with the same thought. Claire is so pure and upright: she would never suspect without good reason! There were at least some appearances —! One day, Claire came to me, it was six months ago — when my suspicions were strongest — I was terribly tormented, I spied on your father, even.— She told me she was tired of Hélène's company, that they didn't get along well together, that she would be glad to get rid of her. Of course she didn't tell me her suspicions in so many words: a young girl like that! Then I couldn't question her, you understand! Well, I was at my wits' end. I might have risked my own peace of mind, but to expose my daughter to *that* — the day after, Mademoiselle Vatrin left.

ROBERT. We weren't careful enough. Claire is very sensitive and proud, and I shouldn't like her to have found out about us — You see, *we* are the ones!

DUCHESS. Yes, thank Heaven! But Claire changed toward her father just as I did, from that time on. Haven't you noticed how formal and distant she is toward him! She never says nice things to him, nor gives him little surprises as she used to! She is even rather impudent at times!

ROBERT. Yes, I've noticed. Perhaps we can insinuate that she was on the wrong scent.

DUCHESS. We must try, yes! I love your father deeply, and my first duty is to make you respect him. We must forget what I've said here — it was an insult to him —. I shall remember only one thing: my almost scandalous joy in finding out my mistake.

ROBERT [*seriously*]. Mother, it is to our interest to forget these things — [*After a pause, in a low tone.*] I still want to ask you for that promise. It is this: I want to see Hélène once more before I die. Let her come here. I admit, I'm asking a great deal, but —

DUCHESS. It is a great deal! Do you mean — ? Mademoiselle Vatrin, your — Mademoiselle Vatrin under our roof? What if Claire should meet her and they should talk — ! Claire, your own sister! Just think!

ROBERT. Do you imagine that I should ask you without considering the whole matter? I confess it's a mad idea, but I must see her. If you refuse, I'll go to her.

DUCHESS. You! To her!? In your state, all alone! It would be your death!

ROBERT [*excitedly*]. A few weeks more or less will make very little difference! I beg you, let her come! Not only must I see her, but you must welcome her yourself!

DUCHESS [*with determination*]. No! You mustn't think of it!

ROBERT. She is the mother of my son —

DUCHESS [*thunderstruck*]. A son! My God, Robert, what are you telling me?! A son!

ROBERT [*rather warmly*]. Having no personal fortune, I can't leave them anything. Hélène's life and the child's are therefore at your mercy. I confide them to your care — my son! Think, Mother, where yours will be before long! Treat mine a little as you would your own! —

[*He stops, gasping for breath, his hand on his chest.*]

DUCHESS [*holding back the tears*]. Rest, Robert! We'll send your sister away for a day or two: your father will take her! Mademoiselle Vatrin may come then, I shall treat her well. The child — Oh, if I had suspected that when I was so tormented about your father I couldn't have stood it all! When was he born?

ROBERT. Two months ago — at Paris.

DUCHESS [*hesitating*]. What —? Under what name? I don't know what they do in such a case? I mean, how did they name the child?

ROBERT [*surprised*]. Why, Vatrin, of course, like his mother.— Now, my duty is to make provision for their future. I beg you on my knees to do this — But to call him anything but Vatrin —!

DUCHESS [*as if relieved of a great weight*]. Oh, Robert, I can breathe again!

[*Enter the Duke, in hunting costume, followed by a servant who lights a paper torch from the fire, goes out and returns a moment later with two lighted lamps; he goes out once more to get the Duke's slippers. The stage is brightly illuminated.*]

DUKE. Good evening!

DUCHESS. You are late, Henri!

[*She kisses him with great tenderness, at which he is surprised.*]

ROBERT [*inquisitively*]. What did you kill?

DUKE. Don't say anything about that! We had fearful luck! When we got to the wood this morning, we were on the trails of nearly thirty boars. We were going to have the devil of a fine chase!

ROBERT [*impatiently*]. Did you kill anything?

DUKE. A little sow — weighed only a hundred and twenty! I put a bullet through her, and the dogs finished up a quarter of an hour later.

[*Enter the servant, with the Duke's slippers. — The fire burns brightly.*]

DUCHESS. Here are your slippers; you ought to change before the snow melts through your overshoes; look how it's running! You're in a regular puddle!

DUKE [*sitting by the fireplace*]. Lord, what

a splendid fire! That puts life into you! [*He stretches forth his feet, and the servant puts on the slippers.*]

ROBERT. Is it snowing?

DUKE. Hard: the branches of the trees are beginning to break with the weight. We were hard put to find our way this evening.

SERVANT [*rises, takes the boots and leggings, and is about to leave*]. Nicolas the forester wishes to know whether he may see Monsieur?

DUKE [*quickly*]. Yes, yes, in the antechamber; I'll see him —

DUCHESS. Receive him here, why not? There's no reason why you should go running after your foresters, tired as you are!

DUKE. I'm not tired! Very well, then! [*To the servant, annoyed.*] Let him come in here — [*The servant goes out.*]

ROBERT. Wasn't Nicolas with you today?

DUKE [*embarrassed*]. No, he was not.

ROBERT. You'll see: he's had plenty of boars in his section of the forest all day, and he'll want orders for to-morrow.

DUKE. To-morrow is your consultation, you know. I shan't go out.

DUCHESS. We have already had the consultation: this evening.

DUKE. What, without letting us know —?

DUCHESS. Doctor Jaubert telegraphed that he would have to come one day earlier on account of an official ceremony at which he has to speak to-morrow. Because of the storms this side of Sedan, the telegram was delayed. The doctors came quite unexpectedly, you see. We were all so surprised!

DUKE. Well, what did they have to say? How was he?

DUCHESS [*with a gesture of despair*]. Not very well!

DUKE. Ah —!

ROBERT. Not at all well, Father: you and I won't kill many more boars together.

DUKE [*sadly*]. What did they advise?

DUCHESS. Go south as soon as possible.

DUKE. South, where? Pau? Nice? —

DUCHESS. Nice.

[*Enter Nicolas. He stands in the doorway at the back, hat in hand.*]

NICOLAS. It's me, Monsieur le duc —

ROBERT. Good evening, Nicolas, any boars?

NICOLAS [*coming down stage a little*]. No, Monsieur Robert, I've come here on business.

ROBERT. Great hunting weather, isn't it, Nicolas?

NICOLAS [*shaking his head in affirmation*]. Fine, Monsieur Robert. Snow's falling in sheets! If this keeps up, we can't take a dog out, or even a beater!

ROBERT. Seems there's a good many boars about this year, eh?

NICOLAS. Oh, quite a few; nothing to complain of. We had five wolves yesterday at *Bois Brûlé*.

ROBERT. They were howling all night at the end of the pond. I heard them from my bed. [*His eyes glistening.*] Five of them! [*With a sigh.*] Well, that's all over for me, Nicolas —

NICOLAS. Ah, Monsieur Robert, your health isn't —?

ROBERT [*with a bitter laugh*]. Ha! Ha! My health was never better!

DUCHESS [*putting her arm around his neck*]. Come, son, it's nearly time for dinner; let's not keep your father. He must have a terrific appetite. Good evening, Nicolas.

NICOLAS. Good evening, Madame la duchesse. Hope you're better soon, Monsieur Robert!

[*Robert thanks him with a nod, and goes out with his mother.*]

DUKE [*standing with his back to the fire*]. Have you just come from town?

NICOLAS. This instant, Monsieur le duc.

DUKE. Have you seen Mademoiselle Vatrin?

NICOLAS. Yes, Monsieur le duc: I'm afraid Monsieur won't like it!

DUKE. Come, out with it! Did she read my letter?

NICOLAS. Yes, of course, but —

DUKE. Well? What then?

NICOLAS. This: I went as Monsieur told me, to the Hôtel du Cheval-Blanc —

DUKE. With your wife?

NICOLAS. Naturally, because Monsieur explained that we were to take the child from Mademoiselle Vatrin and keep it with us.— Well, my wife was mighty cold traveling all day in this weather — you see, it was only three weeks since she had a baby, and she's still a little weak — Well, I says to her, " What's the matter with you? It's for Monsieur le duc, and his son; can't spare any pains!"—

DUKE. Yes, and was Mademoiselle Vatrin waiting for you?

NICOLAS. That's it. She just got off the train from Paris not a quarter of an hour ago — the snow'd blocked all the trains. You ought to've seen that baby! Lord, he was hungry — like a little dog at his soup, when my wife came, begging Monsieur's pardon —

DUKE. Then he's with you now — is he well?

NICOLAS. Ah, Monsieur can be sure of that! Just now by the fireplace I left him grinning at my wife.

DUKE. Then what are you talking about, saying things aren't going well? It seems to me that everything is perfect?

NICOLAS. Everything's all right for the youngster, but the mother, that's different! When I told her her room was ready, and says to her to tell us a few days ahead when she was coming, so as to have time to get things ready, she answered — well, you ought to have heard her! — she didn't want the room; she wasn't coming more than two or three times a year, and stay for an hour or so just to see the baby, and she'd come when she liked, without letting us know ahead of time. You could have knocked me over with a feather to hear her talk the way she did; 'specially as Monsieur le duc had the idea she was going to stay four or five days each time. So I says to her, "Wait a minute! Perhaps Mademoiselle doesn't remember that the house is in the middle of the wood, no one hardly ever comes here, and you could live here all year and be safe. If my wife and I don't go around telling tales, the squirrels'll be the only ones to know the secret!" And she says to me, "I remember the house. I've been there often enough, on my walks — the air is good for my son — I don't know what you mean by the rest —" That's what she said, Monsieur le duc. — I think she's leading you a merry chase, as they say. I don't think that's nice of her, a bit. I don't think either that things are going the way Monsieur le duc wanted 'em to go, about her room and all that.

DUKE. Did she send a letter?

NICOLAS. No. Only she said she was going back to Paris to-night.

DUKE. Very well — I'll arrange to come and see you to-morrow. [*As Nicolas is about to go the Duke intercepts him.*] Tell me, he's good-looking — the youngster?

NICOLAS. Oh, yes! Should have heard my wife when she was undressing him — fine set-up! — Not a thing the matter with him —!

DUKE [*smiling*]. And his face?

NICOLAS [*laughing*]. His face! Oh, if I dared talk about that to Monsieur le duc, but if Monsieur begins —! Well, Monsieur, I'd like to see Monsieur put his face next to the youngster's. People'll see the resemblance right off —

DUKE [*in a revery*]. Take good care of him! Good evening!

[*Nicolas goes out.*]

[*Enter the Duchess.*]

DUKE. So he's worse?

DUCHESS [*goes to the Duke, and takes his hand with great feeling*]. Worse than we imagine, dear!

DUKE [*with concentrated rage*]. Are we going to stand by with folded arms? Can't we do something? There are plenty of new remedies — some of them kill at once, but there are some that are absolutely miraculous!

DUCHESS. Nothing short of a miracle can save Robert — his lungs are all eaten away!

DUKE. The last of the Chantemelles! The end of the family!

DUCHESS [*in despair*]. Henri!

DUKE. You know how I take those things to heart! Others don't attach so much importance to them! But that makes no difference to me! Let me mourn for our whole race in my only son — my son!

DUCHESS. I can think only of him — poor child! It wasn't so very long ago that he was running about the park in short trousers. I remember how he used to come in with his burning red cheeks, and his legs scratched by the thistles — [*She sobs.*] So upright, and noble, and proud!

DUKE. He is a worthy close to our glorious line: Robert de Chantemelle! He is the last of us! The line will be dead! [*He accents this last word in so strange a manner, that the Duchess quivers. They exchange glances.*]

DUCHESS. Dead! [*A pause.*] Henri, why do you look at me that way? Do you know — something?

DUKE. Something? What, Anne? What are you alluding to?

DUCHESS. I? I alluded to nothing, it was you — Robert hasn't the slightest suspicion that you know his secret —

DUKE [*angrily*]. I don't know anything about it. Speak, tell me whether he has been saying anything!

DUCHESS. Robert has a son.

DUKE. What are you —? Robert, a son! — And the mother —?

DUCHESS. Hélène Vatrin —

DUKE. Do you mean —? Are you sure?

DUCHESS. Robert told me so just now.

DUKE [*his eyes flashing, his fists clenched, crosses to the other side of the stage*]. The damned prostitute! And Robert! Damned —! If he wasn't already half dead, I'd —

DUCHESS [*terror-stricken, throws herself into the Duke's arms, and prevents his going to find Robert*]. Henri! Henri! It's horrible! Henri, you're not yourself!

DUKE. Beautiful goings-on in this house! They were very, very lucky I didn't discover them —!

DUCHESS. Henri, for Heaven's sake, be calm — a scene with Robert would kill him!

DUKE. I'll spare him, but her —! She's a — a —

DUCHESS. She? A poor inexperienced young girl we exposed to danger, little thinking — We left her free all day long with a young man about — it was perfect folly! When I think —! I thought I was doing her a favor, and I was the cause of her ruin —

DUKE. Damned women, with their sensitiveness! No, of course, you find her very interesting! — You don't seem to remember that Robert was with her at the very time the doctors ordered him to be most careful! We wondered why he — Your dear little protégée!

DUCHESS. Henri, I refuse to argue about it, unless you talk more calmly. You are entirely unjust. Hélène came to us a pure girl; if she leaves ruined, whose fault is it? It's not at all generous of you to treat her the way you do, in order to escape all the responsibility!

DUKE [*after a pause*]. Very well! There was something inevitable in it all! Of course, she may have some excuse — those long walks with Robert — we must have been blind!

DUCHESS. We must have.— We owe something to her now.

DUKE [*scowling*]. What?

DUCHESS. If not to her, to Robert's son; you don't intend to abandon him, do you?

DUKE [*pensively*]. Robert's son!

DUCHESS. It is no more than just that we should look after him.

DUKE. Of course! His son — his — where is he?

DUCHESS. With his mother, doubtless, in Paris.

DUKE [*considering, half-smiling*]. In Paris — Don't you feel as if you'd like to — kiss him? Good Lord, he's Robert's son, after all!

DUCHESS. You are very good at bottom, dear! Now I am ready to tell you of the promise Robert induced me make to him. He wants to see Hélène once more before he dies! I consented, because I was sure you would let him — [*Gesture from the Duke.*] Will you?

DUKE [*quickly*]. Very well, very well, it's not a matter of great importance — [*He walks about the room.*] Let her come — she may stay as long as she likes, or go, or hang herself, for all I care! I'm interested in the child! [*Standing before his wife, his arms crossed.*] Then Robert is not the last of the Chantemelles!

DUCHESS. You admit that the other —?

DUKE. Whether I admit it or not, he is!

DUCHESS. You forget, the mother —

DUKE. Nothing! But now I come to think about it, she's not so bad; the fact that she —

DUCHESS. She might cause us a great deal of trouble if she tried to force Robert to marry her — but luckily, she is not thinking of doing that. My talk with Robert led me to believe that she is really quite sensitive on the point. Then Robert wouldn't think of marrying her.

DUKE [*bruskly*]. He might consider it, though —

DUCHESS [*surprised*]. What?

DUKE. Does this marriage seem something to be avoided at any cost?

DUCHESS. Henri, you frighten me. Five minutes ago, you were fearfully angry — you were terrible — now you are joking! This is not the time for that!

DUKE. I was angry five minutes ago, but what leads you to suppose I am not now? At least, I am not joking.

DUCHESS. Then you are serious? It's ridiculous! I admit, Hélène is a nice, intelligent, presentable girl —

DUKE [*breaking forth*]. Still she's only Hélène, with all her niceness, and intelligence — I don't care about that! She has made you a grandmother; keep that in mind, and then agree with me that we ought to marry them.

DUCHESS. Ought to —!

DUKE. For the sake of the child! To make him legally what he really is: a Chantemelle!

DUCHESS. Henri, don't do it! Think of Mademoiselle Vatrin as Claire's sister! Oh, no!

DUKE. It's not pleasant to think about — by any means! — But what can we do? We shall both suffer, you and I — I more than you. I have always wanted a grandson — and now I've found him, I take him —

DUCHESS. Pick him up! Find him!!

DUKE [*getting angry*]. That's enough! I want to — and when I say " I want," I'm determined to have —!

DUCHESS. My wishes never had very much influence with you — *I* always wanted to live somewhere else! If you had consented to leave your woods and live for part of the year in Paris, Claire might have gone into society, chosen a husband, and not have been exposed to all this —! Mademoiselle Vatrin would never have set foot in the house, and Robert, instead of burying himself in the country and brooding over the past, would probably have married, and you wouldn't have been forced to pick up a grandson off the streets —

DUKE. Charming! I am to blame for everything! I'm to blame for Robert's sickness! Well, if my will has been the cause of evil, it's now about to make reparation: Robert will marry Mademoiselle Vatrin, take that as final. I'm not going to allow any woman to influence me in a matter of this kind!

DUCHESS. Luckily Robert has a will of his own. He sees this matter in the same light as I do, and you can't domineer over him as you can me: he's a man!

DUKE. He will consent.

DUCHESS. No!

DUKE. Here he is; let him decide.

[*Enter Robert.*]

DUKE [*approaching him, his hands folded behind his back*]. Ah, you gay young bird!

ROBERT [*astonished*]. Father!

DUKE [*good-humoredly*]. I hear fine news about you! A great surprise for your old father [*With a slight menace in his words.*] who ought to shoot you —

DUCHESS. Henri!

DUKE. But I shan't! I have something else to consider now. [*Seriously.*] You have a son. I thank you from the bottom of my heart for perpetuating the family line, just at the moment when it seemed about to end. Your son! I claim him in order that our name shall survive: I am old and you are — not well. At the same time, I shall ask you to make a sacrifice — a big sacrifice, for I know your — what people call — prejudice.

ROBERT. You want me to marry Hélène? I thought of that when I used to plan how to perpetuate the family name —

DUKE. Well?

ROBERT. Well, I love Hélène —

DUKE [*fiercely*]. I don't see how that detail makes it more difficult!

ROBERT. It does. You treat this marriage as a business transaction. Now, in considering your proposal, I am thinking of the future of the woman I love. Can you imagine her between Mother and Claire? — The day she feels she is not absolutely an equal among you, I shall take her away.

DUKE. Your wife *will* be an equal!

ROBERT. I am ready to marry her. I don't think I owe you any thanks — my happiness has nothing to do with this. We all want only one thing —

DUCHESS. Not I, Robert! Your father spoke of sacrifice; well, the real sacrifice will be for Claire and me.

DUKE [*with hauteur*]. You have no idea what you are talking of!

DUCHESS. You are both against me! I consent, then, but let us say nothing more this evening. — My daughter's companion her equal! Oh, no! I hadn't thought of that!

[*She goes out in high indignation.*]

ROBERT. I'll follow her and give her to understand that there's nothing selfish in what I am doing —

DUKE. Go, and don't let her say anything to Claire; we shall let her know at the last minute — Two women in high dudgeon together — !

ROBERT [*smiling*]. Ah, I should think so! [*He goes out.*]

DUKE [*following him with his eyes*]. If he

only knew! Well, he would kill me, but he would think all the same that I govern my house with admirable foresight. And to think of that little fellow, how quickly, how completely he has changed the fate of this family! A crime? Perhaps! We must not do things by halves, and the old must help as well as the young! What difference whose is the child? Our blood runs in his veins, and I can ask no more!

[CURTAIN.]

ACT II

[*Same scene as in the first act. Through the windows are seen a winter landscape, with a bright sun shining upon it, a French garden covered with snow, straight paths bordered by dark evergreens, the branches of which are dotted with tufts of snow. The statues are encased in a thin crust of ice; the water in the basin of the fountain is frozen, but the fountain itself is running. Icicles cling to the sides of the spout. In the distance is the forest tinged with frost and snow, and glistening in the sun.*

As the curtain rises, Robert is alone, waiting near a window. He is carefully dressed, and wears a flower. There is nothing indicative of the negligent patient in his appearance. After a few moments Claire enters, goes straight to her brother, controlling her feelings, which are apparently very turbulent.]

CLAIRE. Robert, I know whom you are waiting for: Mother has just been to my room — now I see why you have been so mysterious these past two days! To think that you are going to marry Hélène! Oh, Robert!

ROBERT. Did Mother tell you why I am doing so?

CLAIRE. Of course! But to tell me that, after I had Hélène sent away! Poor Mother! She murmured something about your loving that woman, that they would consent to let you marry her — then she burst out crying and went away. I did not follow her to get further details. Robert, I used to have great respect for you, for your strength of character; you can have no idea how hurt I am to hear this!

ROBERT. My dear little Claire, Hélène will be here in a quarter of an hour — perhaps sooner: a sleigh travels quickly in this weather — I'm not very strong — let me be in peace until she comes; she mustn't find me stretched out on the sofa, gasping for breath. That's what will happen if I am the least bit over-excited.

CLAIRE. You can't get rid of me so easily as that! I should be a very poor sister if I allowed you to do what you wish, merely to avoid giving you a little pain. You are not going to marry Hélène!

ROBERT. But Father wishes me to!

CLAIRE [*with horror*]. He does! He must be a fool! Give me a reason, at least! I defy you, Father especially! I see I can wait for my reasons! Do you know why Father wants you to? Do you?

ROBERT. Do *you?*

CLAIRE [*in a choked voice*]. Oh — I — what shall I say? —

ROBERT. Father wants me to marry because he cannot bear the idea of seeing me end the line of Chantemelle!

CLAIRE [*embarrassed, to herself*]. It's only a pretense! [*To Robert.*] Couldn't you just as well marry someone else?

ROBERT. I love *her!*

CLAIRE. Poor Robert!

ROBERT. And she loves me! Otherwise, she would never think of marrying me!

CLAIRE. She hasn't a sou, she has no — scruples —

ROBERT. You are very unjust — and besides, it's useless to try to persuade me. Even if Hélène did deserve a little of what you hold against her, I should marry her all the same. It happens that the sacrifice is pleasant to me. That is all!

CLAIRE. A sacrifice for the sake of the family?

ROBERT. Yes, *you* should be able to understand that!

CLAIRE. Every one has his own ideas about family pride.

ROBERT. Oh!

CLAIRE. Our families! See how well they are treated nowadays! To have conquered provinces for the country, to have governed them for centuries, and then to lose every bit of influence — why, Father can't even elect himself mayor of the town here! How humiliating! And what you must have suffered not to have been able to work for the glory of your land! How I pity you, when I see you so inconsolable! And now you marry Hélène Vatrin in order to transmit to your children the creeds and ideas of us mummies!

ROBERT [*crying out*]. Claire! Give me at least the credit of believing that in the face of death I know what I'm doing! I firmly believe that in spite of this inferior alliance, our family is worth perpetuating. This Duke de Chantemelle is nothing: ambassador, minister, prefect — nothing. I am going to marry Hélène because I am positive that the country would otherwise lose a living and valuable force — if the Dukes of Chantemelle disappeared from the face of the earth —

CLAIRE [*ironically*]. I should not be at all surprised if you had made that discovery since you fell in love with Hélène!

ROBERT. It makes no difference if I did, so long as it is true.

CLAIRE [*ironically*]. Are we really of some use?

ROBERT. Yes, because we are well-born. Moral heredity is an incontestable fact. Centuries of military bravery, intellectual culture, refinement, ought surely to produce the very best sort of men and women. Nobility is not a prejudice: the aristocracy is a museum of all that is best in chivalry!

CLAIRE [*bitterly*]. A museum as isolated as a hospital!

ROBERT. That spreads the contagion of devotion! Disinterested science, for example, the sort that has nothing to do with dividends, exists only among the aristocrats. In the United States, there are wonderful inventors, but they have only one end in view: to get as much money as possible! We must look to Europe, with its atmosphere of the old aristocracy, to see great geniuses devoting their lives to the good of humanity! And to think that the crude and simple chivalry of the Middle Age was all the time preparing for the glorious poverty of the great thinkers of to-day! Granted even that this is an exaggeration, the whole idea is at least compatible with modern life. Do we amount to nothing then in the France of to-day? No, if we are forgotten and neglected and despised, we at least repay ingratitude by showing the true spirit of resignation!

CLAIRE [*inspired by Robert's words*]. How true! How splendid! We *are* something! The poor live only because of us; we are not useful in politics, but we know how to console those who deny our very existence! When the Fatherland is in trouble, there is no question about the nobility — those little marquis' who know nothing except how to hunt and dance! Robert, you are right, we still have a part to play!

ROBERT. Forgive me then for wanting to live! Not myself, but in my race!

CLAIRE. You have taught me what we owe to the race, to our family. I was born in a hunting-lodge. How often have you argued with me, gently, never annoyed with me, about the breeding of your dogs and horses: you ought at least then to have the same respect for your family! You should want to live as you say you do, in your son, but you must live too for your own sake: for the sake of this body of yours, worn out by discouragement. You need the strength and the will to be useful even now! Let me receive Hélène first. Don't worry, I know exactly what to say to her! Ten minutes later, she will be gone, for ever. Then we'll save you.

ROBERT. Why do you say you will save me? I have only one hope, but not what you think. In my future there is a tiny ray of brightness — a single ray! Tell me, what if our long empty hallways resounded with the cry of a child, wouldn't you be happy? I am, even to think of it! Tell me, doesn't your instinct —?

CLAIRE [*seriously*]. I did not come here to talk about instinct! I know whom to speak to now; I'm wasting my breath here!

[*Enter the Duke and Duchess.*]

DUKE [*to Robert and Claire*]. A little tiff?

ROBERT [*to the Duke*]. She is giving me some plain advice about my marriage; I am not at all satisfied with her attitude. Mother must have told her everything. She just now refused to discuss the matter further with me. She intends to talk with you. Tell her that in marrying Hélène I am acting according to your wishes. [*Claire listens in terror.*] Mother, stay with me: I want Hélène to see the expression on my face when she comes: the façade of the House of Chantemelle must present a cheerful appearance.

DUCHESS [*while Robert goes to the window*]. I am so glad to see him happy!

[*She joins Robert, and both watch for Hélène.*]

DUKE [*to Claire*]. What Robert says is true: he is going to marry because I want him to.

CLAIRE [*in an undertone*]. This is more horrible than I had ever imagined!

DUKE. What's the trouble?

CLAIRE [*indicating Robert*]. I shan't tell you here: come to my room! You will take pity on him, or me —

DUKE. Go to your room, I will follow you in a moment.

CLAIRE. This is my last word: before this evening, one of us will have sent Mademoiselle Vatrin out of the house; I hope it will be you!

[*She goes out, leaving the Duke petrified. First he goes to the fireplace, then returns to follow Claire, then hesitates, looking toward his wife and son. Robert calls to him.*]

ROBERT. Listen! The bells! It's she!

[*The sound of approaching sleigh-bells is heard outside.*]

DUKE [*going to the window*]. I do hear — yes —

ROBERT [*his face close to the window*]. Why can't we see? There is nothing so far as the eye can reach across the snow.

DUKE. She is coming from the wood — you'll see her turn when she comes around by the stables —

ROBERT. Why the wood? It's much longer that way?

DUKE. I wanted to give you a little surprise, a present for not having written to her, and for allowing your parents to inform her of the state of affairs! She is coming from the forester's cottage, where she has left the child with Nicolas' wife, who has just recently had a child — she is going to nurse the little fellow. Nicolas and his wife are splendid people and can keep the secret —

ROBERT [*interrupting*]. It was very good of you! I'm going to see him —

DUKE [*intercepts him*]. Do me the favor of coming with your mother into the billiard-room — wait until I call you. As head of the family I wish to be the first to receive Mademoiselle Vatrin: she is not yet aware that she is to be your wife. You might appear a little too happy in telling her about it; I shall tell her in quite another manner. Her coming here shall not be a triumphal entry; I am afraid she doesn't yet feel the enormous responsibility that goes with our name, which she will assume so easily. Let me, at the very door of this house, explain what will be expected of her. Then, Robert, she is yours! — Go now —

[*Robert and his mother go out. The Duke looks out of the window an instant, then comes back to meet Hélène.*

Hélène, dressed in a simple traveling suit, enters. She is pretty, but now appears timid and sad. Seeing the Duke, she is about to faint; quivering with emotion, she leans against the door. After a pause, the Duke turns to her.]

DUKE [*dryly*]. Come here! [*She approaches him, very much afraid.*] Yes, it's I! Are you surprised? The child's nurse just told you I had gone away; well, she did as she was told. I wanted to encourage you to come. You see, the Duchess wrote you that Robert was very ill, and authorized you to come — not a word from the Duke — Robert, too, wanted to write, but I did not let him. Now I have a piece of news to announce — Sit down! You're trembling — I'm not angry with you! You don't know what I am going to tell you!

HÉLÈNE [*wringing her hands; in a feeble choked voice*]. Oh, please! I was weak enough to be your mistress almost as soon as I came here. I was only twenty-two, I knew nothing. Monsieur Robert was away then in Palestine; when he came back I fell in love with him — and he knew it!

[*She hides her face.*] Don't despise me! I love him as deeply as a woman can love a man! His love is the only thing that sustained me — I didn't have the strength to leave you! For two years I lived a terrible life — I never saw you that I didn't make up my mind to stop everything — with you, I didn't dare! I waited and waited, too afraid to do anything! Then the baby came, and I had to depend on you. But once I was away, I wasn't afraid of you, and when the forester's wife asked me to stay sometimes with her I had the strength to refuse! You see, I have a little courage left —

DUKE [*brutally*]. What are you talking about? What has Robert's mistress to do with Robert's father? Get rid of that idea! Robert is madly in love with you! Marry him!

HÉLÈNE [*terror-stricken*]. I? Marry Robert?!

DUKE. You must. I want an heir to carry on my name; now I have one! I don't care by what means, but I have one! Never mind who or what you are! You are that heir's mother! You love my son, don't you? You wrote me a letter that was rather touching some time ago, before the child was born, and told me to take care of him in case you died. There was nothing unreasonable in that — of course we should look after the little one. Now we want to make a duke of him — give him our name, our fortune, everything!

HÉLÈNE. There's not only my son to think about, but Robert! He is *your* son, Robert! Do you love him? And yet you talk of this marriage!

DUKE. Robert is my son, but the other is something to me also. Fate demands that I sacrifice one of them. One is young and full of hope, the other we are already mourning — why should I hesitate between the two? Furthermore, I have promised that Robert shall marry you — refuse him now! Can't you see, he will ask you questions; what will you tell him if he learns the truth? Come now, everything is to your advantage: an honorable name for yourself, a title for your son — Robert's son. That little mite is everything! I am willing to kill for his sake, if necessary! Give him to us, for always, irrevocably! Is it a bargain? Don't answer yet! You can't answer! Tell Robert! Meantime, you're in great danger. Somehow, I can't imagine how, Claire has discovered everything. She is opposed to all this. If she says anything, the marriage cannot take place! Robert would be broken-hearted, demand an explanation, and I — Well, what could I answer —?

HÉLÈNE. Then why did I come?

DUKE. Claire doesn't know yet that there *is* a child. She is more concerned with our traditions, our long family line, than any of us, and perhaps she will feel as deeply as I do about perpetuating the name. I shall go and see her now, and in five minutes everything will be arranged.

[*He goes out by the down-stage door. Enter Claire at the back, left. She stops on seeing Hélène.*]

CLAIRE. My father is looking for me, isn't he? [*Hélène makes a vague gesture.*] Mademoiselle, I am glad to have an opportunity of talking with you alone; as we have only a few moments, I shall go straight to the point! Robert is not going to marry you —

HÉLÈNE. I don't ask anything — I want to do what will be best for Robert!

CLAIRE. To save him from disgrace is best for Robert! I know who you are: one evening last summer I was walking by the pond — you were with Father in the boat, and neither of you was any too careful — I was out all that night, a few feet from you — once I was on the point of asking for a place in the boat — I heard things that made my blood run cold. In one second my purity of mind was gone, my respect and affection were killed! That episode has blackened my life. I had you sent away, but I felt just the same as before — the same torture. And now you have come back to poison my life again! Your plan will fail this time: I am going to tell Robert everything!

HÉLÈNE. And kill him!

CLAIRE. He will thank me for sparing him a few days of life in a world where God allows such things to happen!

[*Enter the Duke. He takes in the situation at a glance. He comes and stands between them.*]

DUKE [*with severity*]. Claire, who asked you to come? You ought to have waited until I saw you!

CLAIRE. I changed my mind. I couldn't think clearly then about what you had determined to do.

Even after I considered it, I couldn't understand. I have now given up trying to persuade: I am threatening!

DUKE [*violently*]. Keep still!

CLAIRE. Nothing can make me keep still — my conscience —

DUKE [*with blind fury*]. Keep still, I tell you!! Never mind about your conscience! There are certain things a daughter doesn't say to her father! If you forget yourself again you'll end your days in a convent, or else I'll turn you out of the house —

CLAIRE. I'd rather end my days in a convent, or walk the streets, than breathe this atmosphere of disgrace and shame —!

HÉLÈNE. Monsieur le duc, I ought to leave; I am willing not to see Robert, to be sent away — I am willing — Only let Mademoiselle spare her brother, and help you explain to him why I am leaving.

DUKE [*after a moment's reflection, to Hélène, sympathetically*]. Let me have a word with her in private! [*Hélène nods. He conducts her to the down-stage door, and sees her out. He then returns to Claire.*] Claire, I give in. For the first time, you have called my authority into question! You have your weapons, you can prevent me from doing what I want to do. I shan't argue further. Only know this: from now on there is no intimacy between us!

CLAIRE. I expect to be unhappy. With my courage —

DUKE. That is your affair. You may as well know what this blow will mean to Robert! Yes, and to all of us! It is not hard to accuse your father, and tell him how disgusted you are; you're hardly more than a little boarding-school miss — your mother was unwise enough to tell you everything, a child of your age! I am now talking to you as I would to a judge, a righter of wrongs: I have nothing to hide from you. Robert has a son by Mademoiselle Vatrin.

CLAIRE [*to herself*]. He! A Son?!

DUKE. Whom we have decided to adopt, make one of the family, in order not to let the line die out. If the child had not lived, Robert would think nothing more about the mother — he would not marry her. For myself, I am opening this house to a woman who bears in her arms a sacred gift; I use the word "sacred" advisedly. I want you to weigh the matter carefully. You blamed Robert for being selfish in the face of death, and you blamed me because I was sacrificing him to I don't know what monstrosities. Every word of that is false. Robert is sacrificed, and so am I, but I haven't the right to consider that for a moment. Both of us are sacrificed, thank God! to an ideal, an ideal which you are as anxious as we to preserve as best we can!

CLAIRE. A son!! Poor Robert! His eyes were filled with tears when he told me how splendid it would be to have the empty corridors filled with the voices of children! And to think I was ignoble enough to appear dissatisfied with him! And the brutal way I answered! That is what he meant when he spoke of instinct! His love as a father! I thought he meant something quite different! How could I have been so mistaken! Sometimes, at night, when I'm sitting by the fire, while the wind whistles outside, and the wolves howl just under the window, all at once clear ringing voices come to me and I wake up holding to my breast the end of a phantom — it is that same instinct — then it goes away — but it is always in Robert! Sometimes I almost go crazy. Now you tell me there *is* a child! It may be near at this moment! Papa, why are you looking at me that way? Is he in the house — now?!

DUKE. Almost: he is with Nicolas — go and see him — I could not resist the temptation —

CLAIRE. Can I? [*Slowly.*] Then it is no longer a dream, a vision! Then I am killing a real child, a child I could take in my arms, a child Robert adores, his own flesh and blood! Oh, if you had only heard him! He wants his son to be perfect in everything, because a noble birth gives one moral superiority! Poor boy! He is forgetting the mother! No, he is not forgetting her, he doesn't know! The mother! Ha, what is her heritage, what does she bring us?

DUKE. What are you talking about? Most of our ancestors were statesmen and celebrated generals; I once dreamed of being great, like them — but I've had to pass my life doing nothing. I have tried to forget myself in hunting! There is nothing like country life to soothe wounded pride! During the war, I was no longer a young man, so that I had to enlist as a simple soldier or else stay home by my own fire-side. I enlisted, looking for great deeds to do and a glorious death; I came home diseased and defeated. I had added nothing to the honor of our name. Now, for God's sake, don't let the line die out! We can still work for the glory of our country, the glory that has been handed down to us, until one day a Chantemelle, more intelligent or more fortunate, shall arise and do honor to us! Don't you feel that basic desire to live, to make some place in the world, to exist afterwards — in others?

CLAIRE [*overcome*]. Oh, Papa! with all my soul!

DUKE. No, you don't! Otherwise you would have pitied me! Robert and I cannot last much longer. Don't, don't take these visions of the future from us!

CLAIRE. You think I am indifferent! I have devoted myself, given up my life because of these terrible agonies I have been going through! [*Bowing her head.*] If you ask pity of me, you must in turn at least pity me! If I am to become your — accomplice, I shall be in a terrible situation — pity me!

DUKE. You an accomplice? In what? You have only to say nothing!

CLAIRE. Isn't that terrible enough? Then I shall have been the cause of this marriage! If I say a word, it will not take place!

DUKE. If it does not take place you will be the executioner of the race!

CLAIRE. That's what tortures me! To put such responsibility on the shoulders of a young girl like me! What will happen to us if I don't tell Robert? His child is our glory, the center of all our ambitions, of our very life, everything! But can we forget the mother? That woman! Can't you see what a hell my life has been because of her? Can't you see how afraid of you all I have been? If she comes back, I shall never live in peace again! Yet I am willing to submit, to be miserable, to bear the weight of shame and responsibility which I have no right to bear. I, the little boarding-school miss! What hope have I? I wish I were dead! I wish I knew what to do!!

DUKE [*solemnly*]. Claire, I swear that you ought to do this: it is your duty to obey the head of your family. Why have I educated you to look back to the glory of our house, if I now ask something unworthy of the past? For that reason, I beg you! On my honor, on the honor of my son who is about to die, I promise you that this marriage will save our name!

CLAIRE. I believe you.

DUKE. Thank you, Claire!

CLAIRE [*going to the door behind which Hélène is waiting*]. Come, Hélène!

[*Enter Hélène.*]

I accept a great responsibility: I shall never abandon the woman who is about to become Robert's wife! I cannot be expected to be a real friend — an affectionate friend — but I promise to be a devoted sister. When you are in trouble come to me. I offer you this in all loyalty, Hélène!

DUKE. Let us go to Robert —!

[*He steps back, allowing Hélène and Claire*

to pass him. Claire allows Hélène to precede her out of the room. Hélène gives evidence of extreme nervousness as the Duke and Claire look at her.

The curtain falls only after the stage is empty and the door closed.]

[CURTAIN.]

ACT III

[*A villa in the neighborhood of Nice, situated in the open country. The scene represents a large room elegantly but rather flashily furnished, the kind usually found in rented houses at seaside resorts. Doors to the right and left. At the back, all the way across the stage is a large bay window, through which the sea appears sparkling under a brilliant sky. To the left, outside, a reef with the foam of waves breaking over it.*

Robert is alone, stretched out on a sofa. His legs are covered with a plaid blanket. He appears to be asleep. Enter Hélène; she closes the door noiselessly and approaches the sofa on tip-toe. Robert opens his eyes and speaks to her without turning his head.]

ROBERT. Is that you, Hélène?

HÉLÈNE [*leaning over him and kissing his forehead*]. Yes. Have you had a nice sleep?

ROBERT. Couldn't close my eyes! I tossed about, thinking, always thinking! That attack yesterday — If my mother hadn't happened to come in the moment I lost consciousness, I should have died — [*Pressing his hand to his lips.*] There's always that taste of blood in my mouth! The hemorrhage there, ready to choke me any moment! — What about this south that was going to cure me? This famous south!

HÉLÈNE. We've been here hardly two weeks! It would be miraculous if already —

ROBERT [*interrupting her*]. My poor girl, our marriage! the first month isn't over yet — [*A long pause, during which he holds her hand pressed to his lips.*] Why didn't they bring Henri this morning? Where is he?

HÉLÈNE. In front of the house, playing in the sand. [*Going toward the window.*] Shall I call and have him brought in?

ROBERT. Later! I have so many things to ask you to take care of! My parents are old, soon you will be the only one left. And you'll need help so badly. [*With an effort.*] And — dearest! It's impossible for me to conceive that your happiness no longer depends on me alone!

HÉLÈNE [*gravely*]. It is in your hands, Robert.

ROBERT. What do you mean?

HÉLÈNE. Listen: I should never have spoken of this unless you had begun. I should have preferred to be miserable till the last. But since you have opened the subject — Please, Robert, arrange matters so that if — if I have to lose you, I can go off with little Henri wherever I wish. I want a home of my own.

ROBERT [*rising*]. Leave the family? Here I was deeply concerned because I was afraid you would be left alone, and now you ask to be!

HÉLÈNE. Without you, do you think I could be anything else but alone? Among these people whom I am afraid of? Yes, afraid! Of the

Duke especially! I should be completely at his mercy! I don't even dare raise my voice against him now! Help me! They despise me!

ROBERT. I have never heard a word from them to cause my wife to be ashamed or humiliated. I should never have allowed it!

HÉLÈNE. Not a word has been spoken! They are forced to treat me as an equal, and they do their duty! They are heroically polite, so polite that when the slightest attention is paid me, I blush with shame!

ROBERT. You don't mean Claire? Claire is very good to you, isn't she?

HÉLÈNE [*ironically*]. To me? Claire?

ROBERT. Don't you think so? If it hadn't been for her, perhaps we should never have been married. Mother thought it her duty to raise every imaginable objection: but Claire made God knows what oath to her, and the objections disappeared. After the ceremony, do you remember how she found occasion — awkwardly enough — to say that she knew of the existence of the child, and that he should not be kept from her any longer out of respect for her? What made my father decide to come ahead here and get this house for us? Who went with him? Who found this hidden retreat, where we can now enjoy peace with our son for a little while? I think we owe pretty nearly everything to Claire!

HÉLÈNE. Do you think she has done all this for my sake? She swallowed her dislike for me for the sake of the baby, because that baby is the future of her family; she would make any sacrifice for that!

ROBERT. Very noble of her! So much the worse for those who disparage her for doing it! The honor of mankind is in itself a small and insignificant handful of sacrifices, but it typifies all that is sublime.

HÉLÈNE [*with dignity*]. Very well, I can't see it in that light! I was born without your ideas, your delicacy of feeling about those things! [*Becoming excited.*] But do they think I have no feelings at all? They make me feel from morning to night that I am an inferior being, and must be treated as such! If I weren't a poor simple fool —! I must stand it all because I *love!*

ROBERT [*in consternation*]. Hélène! The idea! To think you could imagine I was hurting you by what I said! This only goes to show how easily you are offended! My parents don't feel that way about you!

HÉLÈNE [*ironically*]. You think so?

ROBERT. Certainly. Why should Claire and I have different ideas from yours? Does our education, which you had no opportunity of having, make you an inferior creature? We all look into the heavens at night: the stars belong to every one! You might at least humor me, and let me preserve the illusion that keeps me alive! It is true, I *am* proud of my title! They say that riches is merely accumulated labor; well, nobility is merely accumulated honor. Hélène, don't let me think that you despise the nobility: it is your first duty to educate our child to respect it.

HÉLÈNE. My dear, I shall do my full duty by the child, provided he remains my child, and not the child of a tyrannical and jealous clan! Believe me, O Robert! Could I talk so calmly of the time when you won't be with us any longer, if I didn't think I was standing at this moment before the very gates of hell?! Save me! Don't let them drag me back with them to that dreary home, where sad-faced members of the House of Chantemelle live and look like antique armor! I have loved you because you were the only one in that place who had a heart like mine! It would break that heart, Robert, if —

ROBERT. But why should I oppose my authority to theirs? Legally they have no rights over you! They can't force you!

HÉLÈNE. I haven't the courage to resist! If I went back to Chantemelle I should never leave! If I wanted to go away, they would all combine against me, say I perjured myself, and then I should be humble and say nothing — Oh, it would be horrible! Save me from that, Robert!

ROBERT. I am already sorry I made you my nurse! I can't promise you your liberty after you are through with me! I'll put it in my will that you shall live where you like, and I'll tell Claire about it.

HÉLÈNE [*anxiously*]. Why speak to her? She will never agree with you! She will only oppose you and make you worse! Only promise to put that in your will: that will be enough.

ROBERT. Claire is not used to my doing things without consulting her; I couldn't consent to separating you from the family without speaking to her and telling her my reasons for doing so. Don't worry, she may disagree with me as much as she pleases, I shall not give in: you have my word for it!

[*Enter Claire. She has been out-doors, and wears a walking-suit; under her arm is a card-board box.*]

CLAIRE [*taking off her gloves and hat*]. The sun is blinding. I went to the customs office to sketch the reef, but the sea was a perfect blaze! I could hardly see a thing!

HÉLÈNE. What do you find so interesting about the reef? Haven't you already three drawings of it in your album?

CLAIRE. That stone pinnacle which seems to totter when the waves break over it fascinates me! It's like a fisherman standing in the water.

ROBERT. Or a shepherd guarding his sheep. — Look, the flock is jumping about now!

CLAIRE [*smiling*]. Flock?! How common that word would have sounded over there while I was sketching! — I imagined —! That boiling tide — why, even in the calmest weather it seems as if there were creatures beneath it forcing it up, in order to rise up to the sun — Sirens, maybe, who regret the times when they danced and gamboled on the beach! I'm sure they used to live around my rock, those divine cruel creatures!

ROBERT [*laughing*]. Divine? Why? Because they brought poor unfortunate sailors and cabin-boys to their doom?

CLAIRE. I'm afraid so! Yet I think they weren't so dangerous as they are said to be! You remember once how a certain warrior who was on a quest for some Golden Fleece or other, allowed himself to be charmed by their song — and did they make a meal of him? Of course not! They filled him full of good counsels, and conducted him to the island where he found the treasure he was looking for. Another time, among a number of shipwrecked wretches, was an old man who had embarked to go and preach the gospel of Christ Crucified to the savages; in the very teeth of the cannibal goddesses, he made public profession of his faith, and overcame terrible opposition in the midst of the storm — the revelers ate no more that night! The shining bodies and tresses of the Sirens, green with seaweed, triumphantly escorted the missionary to the shore whence he was going to drive the idol; then they — the Sirens — idols themselves, plunged back into the deep and appeared no more.

ROBERT. What imagination! That must be champagne foam around your reef! The sea is positively going to your head!

CLAIRE. Make fun of me, that's right! If the sea makes me romantic, what do the forests do to you? When you come back to Chantemelle after a long trip, the first thing you do is run to the woods, all alone, dressed like a common thief,— and at night to hear you tell what you found by all your dear old hedges —!

ROBERT. Oh, the woods of Chantemelle! How often have I wandered about them! I've never been really happy away from them! But that doesn't prevent my loving the sea! The woods and the sea have a great attraction for me. I have always liked to hunt, and it wasn't the mere killing of animals that I enjoyed: there was something else. It was the thick underbrush, the unknown! I used to listen, tingling with joy, to the moaning of the wind, at first far-off, then rushing on, wave after wave — grandly, mysteriously — and all at once, the tops of the birches would begin to wave high over my head, and the pines and saplings would sway, and I was in the midst of the whirlwind! Then to hear the boars cracking the dry sticks, breaking through hedges — you'd think they were the fauns of old Greece! Then the boar comes out into the opening, a big black thing, hair bristling, tail twisted up in a knot! There *is* your faun! And the light tread of the wolves over the dead leaves! — Head lowered, ears alert, digging round some briar — he looks up, and then vanishes Heaven knows where. And then the lantern reflections of the foxes over the snow! Oh, to think of all that now!

HÉLÈNE [*seated a little distance from him, and trying to attract attention to herself*]. Yes, you prefer the forests to the sea!

ROBERT. I like both, but not in the same way. The aristocrat in me loves those old trees, as old as we are, that spread their protecting arms over the multitudes. Are we not the brothers of the pines and giant hemlocks? I never wander about among them without assuming their splendid attitude of arrogance. I soar high above the fields, drink in the light and the pure air and proudly scatter acorns and pine-nuts to the famished countryside.— Here by the sea another being awakes within me; the waves come in never-ending procession and break on the beach, each decked out in diamonds by the sun — small in calm weather, gigantic in the storm. Then I say to myself, " Here is a far different image of mankind from what I get in the forests." The uniformity of those waves, bearing forever the burden of the fleets of the world, those waves that are doomed to eternal unrest — there is something monotonous in all that, too monotonous for my forester's instinct! Then I wonder whether men can ever make their way through life like the waves, without jostling, wrangling, and hurting one another. Then I am seized with fear: I am afraid that the wave of humanity, if all men are made equal, like the waves of the sea, will continue to rise up and up, mysteriously attracted from above! — Here I am, part forester, part man of the sea — the trees and the hedges and the waves!

CLAIRE. Oh, Robert, how truly we are brother and sister! From birth we have been buried in the old château, discouraged because we had nothing to do, looking to the winds and the woods, the waves and the clouds to sing us the song of life. I never read much, but I have heard it said that everything nowadays is bad; yet these forces in nature paint for me the life of the past. You, you question them for the future — which of us is right?

ROBERT [*facing Claire*]. I! To speak of the future and to die to-morrow is futile enough; but I have a son, and I live in agony wondering what his destiny will be. Poor little one, I fear I have given him a mournful heritage in taking him into this family! Will he have a place of his own to breathe in and think, as I never had? No, I never had that, even at Chantemelle! I have loved you all, but I was never able to talk with you without getting into a dispute — oh, that eternal wrangling! [*Smiling.*] I became a Socialist to spite Father, a Freethinker to spite Mother, a Republican to spite you — and the whole thing ended in recriminations! When I went to Paris to complete my studies, I was again wofully out of place: nearly all my fellow-students held radically different views from ours. *I* ought to have been able to get along with them — but I couldn't! I was more dogmatic with them than Father is with us, more religious than Mother, more Royalist than you. There are *déclassés* of high rank, as well as of low — I am one of the former. I am intellectually in sympathy with the present generation, but my heart is with the past! Wherever I go, half of me is an exile. I must save my son from this torture!

CLAIRE. Of course you must! He will never be like you, who never dared be yourself except alone with your books, who were afraid that the living might perceive in you a radical, a revolutionist against the family! He will keep up with his times,— I am even willing to bury my dislikes and become modern in order to be with him myself. But you will not object, will you, to my keeping my old pride deep down in my heart? I shall explain to him later all your ideas about the nobility: the source of true chivalry!

ROBERT. In the joy of being a father, I had hoped for that, and I finally brought you to think as I did. But these last few days I have been discouraged — I have to come down to earth again! It may be that my sickness makes me believe I foresee the downfall of all our family, while only *I* am dying. No matter! I'm only too glad not to have to explain to my son all the doubts that have arisen in me: that awful past that seems like a drag on our future! I confide him to you, who are tall and dignified like the pines, healthy and clear-seeing! My son will have only to look about him to find the finest examples of honor and bigness of spirit: Father is loyalty and probity incarnate, and you would never tell a lie even to save your life!

CLAIRE [*agitated*]. You may be sure of me: I shall look after your son so well that not the shadow of a base thought can reach him.

HÉLÈNE [*goes to Robert, takes him aside, and speaks to him.*] Oh, Robert! To confide our son to the family before me, after your promise! I thought I could trust you, Robert!

ROBERT [*aside to Hélène*]. Oh, I'm terribly sorry! Forgive me, Hélène! You have my word, and you may depend upon it more than ever!

HÉLÈNE [*shrugging her shoulders, as she goes to the window*]. There, I hear him crying! [*Looking out the window.*] Oh, that nurse! — Talk ahead about your grand ideas, Mama is going to look after baby!

[*She takes a garden-hat from the rack and goes out.*]

ROBERT [*going to Claire*]. Claire, Claire, you speak about little Henri as if he had no mother! There, you see, she's the one who really takes care of him!

CLAIRE [*smiling*]. Robert, you are to blame! You tell us what you want done with the boy, and you always speak to me about it in his mother's presence.

ROBERT. I didn't mean to do that. I was speaking to you both. But you are not kind to Hélène. What's the matter? Hélène has been telling me that after I'm gone it will be impossible for her to live with you. She means to settle where she will not be humiliated later on in the presence of her son.

CLAIRE [*astonished*]. She wants to take the child away? Did she say that? What did you say?

ROBERT. I'm sorry, but I told her she was right. In my will, I shall make provision for her to live independently.

CLAIRE [*at her wits' end*]. Robert, don't do that!

ROBERT. I promised her.

CLAIRE. Don't do it!

ROBERT. Claire, I am as sorry as you are to have the child taken from the hereditary home; there are certain sacred things I should have liked him to grow up to feel; but you can't expect a woman of Hélène's age to remain buried alive for the rest of her life! The moment she suffers from your contact, and says she does, I want her to be left free. Won't she be free anyway? I shall ask her, beg her, to stay at Chantemelle, but who can force her against her wishes? In a year's time, she might leave you, hating and despising you all — all you have to do is make her wish to be with you, by love, by affection.

CLAIRE. Whatever you do, leave us the child! Listen to me: I tell you, this is a matter of the gravest importance!

ROBERT. Let you have the child?! I once asked you to take him, and you refused; now *I* refuse! The child belongs to his mother, and if Hélène consents to abandon him, then I should be the first — Why —!

CLAIRE. To have a Duke of Chantemelle educated by Hélène Vatrin — to have him grow up with her ideas, out of sympathy with our beliefs, our faith?! Would you allow that? To think that a creature like Hélène could so deceive you —! Now I see what you meant when you spoke about the uniformity of the waves and the vision of a new mankind! Her ideas, the ideas of a woman of the common people have taken root in you! You try to make those ideas fit in with your own, you are blinded because they please you — you are infected with them! Robert, come to yourself! Before your marriage, you swore to me that if Hélène were not the mother of your child, you would not marry her! Now you are sacrificing your son to her!

ROBERT. Very well, admit that I am; you forget one thing: our parents are getting old. Hélène will of necessity be the only one left to take care of her son! *There's* the sacrifice!

CLAIRE. I am young, and I am stronger than Hélène! I offer my whole life, Robert, for your son.

ROBERT [*struggling to dominate his emotion*]. Impossible!

CLAIRE. Then why did you speak to me, and me alone,— not long ago,— when you were telling how the future Duke de Chantemelle ought to be educated? Wasn't I the only one who understood?

ROBERT. Stop it!

CLAIRE. Then in your opinion Hélène is my equal?

ROBERT. Claire, you are prejudiced against Hélène; and you have a right to judge: your life has been spotless. But you must look at things from a different point of view. You are no longer a little girl. Remember, a woman may make a slip and yet remain worthy of respect: Hélène is such a woman.

CLAIRE. Don't leave your son with her!

ROBERT. Oh —! Well?

CLAIRE. Remember, Robert, remember, Mademoiselle Vatrin was dismissed from Chantemelle for misbehavior —

ROBERT. She loved me!

CLAIRE [*driven to despair*]. Loved — everybody!!

[*Enter the Duke, from one of the rooms at the side.*]

DUKE. Claire, are you mad? You shout —! I heard you from the smoking-room. You know what the doctors say? You, too, Robert?

CLAIRE. We are facing a greater danger than that! Father, I was willing, as you were, for Robert to marry — you know why,— you know what it cost me! That was for the sake of the family, for the future, for Henri: the hope of us all. Well, that's over now, we have only to look at the wreckage — and regret what we have done. Why didn't we think of one simple thing, that Henri before belonging to us belongs to his mother? And last of all, here is Robert who is going to make provision in his will for Hélène to leave us and take away her child!

DUKE [*to Robert*]. Is this true?

ROBERT. Yes.

DUKE. Don't do it!

ROBERT. It is my right.

DUKE. It is! But don't do it!

ROBERT. Give me a reason.

DUKE. A thousand, if you like.

CLAIRE [*to the Duke*]. I have told him — all I could tell him!

DUKE. There are others! Hélène's origin, for instance — of course, we don't wish to reproach her —! Things are done in these days that make the blood run cold! Even if ours were the most obscure of names, I should still say, save our honor: don't leave it in the hands of that woman!

ROBERT. I refuse to allow you to insult Hélène!

DUKE [*rising to his full height*]. You refuse?!

ROBERT [*making a great effort*]. I am weak, but you cannot bend me. If you say a single insulting word against her, I'll leave the house and take her with me!

DUKE. She is now out there in the garden;

let her come in and talk to me, face to face, about her rights! Let her dare! Let her —!

CLAIRE. She will be a little less proud then!

ROBERT. She will come here, to pack the trunks and follow me!

DUKE. I shall keep the child, in spite of his mother.

ROBERT. He is mine!

DUKE. Ours!

ROBERT. Mine!

DUKE [*menacing*]. Ours!

CLAIRE [*frightened*]. Father! Listen to me!

DUKE [*thrusting Claire aside*]. You go away! This is between us!

CLAIRE. Father!

DUKE. Go!

[*He takes Claire by the shoulders, and thrusts her out of the room. She remains behind the door, however, which is not quite closed.*]

DUKE [*goes quickly to Robert, overcome with rage*]. Now! She was mine before she was yours! I committed the crime of letting you marry her in order that the family might not die out with you! I don't intend to let you take from us the child we have all paid so dearly for! He belongs to the family; I forbid you to lay hands on him! There! I think that is all! [*Suddenly calm and dignified.*] Now, if you think I should die, I am ready.

ROBERT [*looks his father in the eyes for a long time, then walks with unsteady steps toward the door. As he is about to leave, he summons up all his reserve strength*]. One of us has to die!

[*He goes out, tottering. Claire is seen behind the door; she receives him in her arms.*]

DUKE [*going to the window and calling*]. Hélène, come here!

HÉLÈNE [*outside*]. Why? It's so lovely outdoors.

DUKE [*stamping on the floor*]. Come here! [*In a voice of thunder.*] I tell you, come here!

[*He returns to the center of the room, and stands waiting, his eyes fixed upon the door. Enter Hélène; the moment she sees the expression on the Duke's face, she is terror-stricken.*]

DUKE [*bruskly*]. You have tried to steal our child! — You bear one of the most honorable names in France, you are rich and respected — you ought to be satisfied. You have asked for more, and you will now receive justice. I have told everything to Robert.

HÉLÈNE [*sobbing*]. My God!

DUKE. My words have sacrificed a life: either Robert's or mine — I don't know which. I told Robert I was willing to die — he said that one of us *must,* and he is right. He is now trying to find a way that will avoid all scandal, and he will succeed, I know he will!

[*Enter Claire. The Duke questions her with a look.*]

CLAIRE. He says nothing! I wanted to talk with him — he gave me such a look — ! I didn't dare stay with him! He knows that I knew everything — !

DUKE. Repeat it to him, word for word;

don't leave him! The only honor in my crime is that you, the soul of purity, are my accomplice! Go and tell him: he must not have the shadow of a doubt!

[*Enter the Duchess.*]

DUCHESS. What has happened? Robert is terribly changed! I found him nearly dead in a chair! When he saw me, he got up and told me he was leaving for Chantemelle to-night. I couldn't argue with him!

CLAIRE [*going to the Duke, and looking him straight in the face*]. That will kill him! It was twenty degrees below zero there yesterday!

DUCHESS. I told him, but he wouldn't listen. I told him I would find Hélène for him, and his face was —! Now I remember, the moment I pronounced Hélène's name, he turned white as snow! We can't let him go away like that! Hélène, why aren't you with him now?

HÉLÈNE [*in terror*]. No, no, not now! No!

DUCHESS. Have you and Robert —? Only this morning you were talking together — What's the matter?

[*Hélène gives a vague gesture.*]

DUKE. Hélène had better stay here! You see she is very nervous. She's not well! She can't go to him!!

DUCHESS [*to the Duke*]. Then you speak to Robert, you have so much influence with him!

DUKE [*hesitating*]. I? I can't go! [*Glancing at Claire significantly*]. Claire, you ought to speak to him.

DUCHESS. But why not you, Henri? Why, you are nearly as pale as Hélène! Are you afraid of something? You, too, Claire! Your face is changed!

CLAIRE. There's nothing strange, Mother! I am afraid for Robert!

DUCHESS. Why do you look at your father that way? What's the matter? You are hiding something from me, all of you! There is some secret — what is it? Am I the only one in the house not to know? Hélène, tell me! [*Hélène hides her face in her hands, sobbing, as the Duchess looks at her in silence.*] Hélène, this is not the first time I have asked you a question — the last time you behaved as you do now —. Cry, cry now, if you like, but you are going to tell me!

DUKE. Never mind her, I'll answer for her!

CLAIRE [*terrified*]. Let me tell her!

DUCHESS. You, Claire? Last summer you begged me to send her away from Chantemelle; you gave me no reasons, and I asked for none. We were face to face, both of us quivering with fear. Your eyes spoke — spoke and told me — what Robert has just found out! It's too horrible! Such shame in our house! And *she* has married our son! And you, Claire, knew all the time! And you never said a word! Oh, I don't know what I —! And you knew —!

CLAIRE. Mother, since I've known this secret, I haven't had a moment's peace of mind — I have sacrificed all to something that is greater than we are —

DUCHESS. Nothing is more sacred than an oath — you have no sense of honor if you believe otherwise!

CLAIRE. I was thinking only of the child.

DUCHESS. The child! Ha! The poorest of peasants cries when he loses his son, and when Robert dies you won't think of him — his son to you is only a title! If the title is saved, you are happy! The child will live in glory and honor, no matter what infamies are committed to save the title! And all for a poor little bastard —

DUKE. Don't insult the child! Robert will not allow it!

DUCHESS. Robert will not —! [*She breaks out into tears.*] Your own son, killed by you — let him decide — don't ask anything of me —

[*Enter Robert, his face deadly pale. He can hardly walk; but he shows great strength in his efforts. As soon as she sees him, the Duchess assumes an attitude of outward calm. Claire goes to him at once, and helps him to walk.*]

ROBERT. Let us forget ourselves for the time being, and save little Henri: he is the family, think of him!

DUCHESS. We'll do anything, only stay with us!

ROBERT. I am going to the Ardennes this evening — I have presentiments, and I am never mistaken about them: this time, I feel that death is not far away, and when it comes I want to be *there*, with my memories of the past: not only of my youth, but of all our glorious past! I feel I have lived for centuries and centuries! The trip will doubtless cut short my life by a few days, but I shall at least have shown you what devotion to an ideal is!

DUKE. An ideal?

ROBERT. Yours, ours: the honor of our name. Hélène and Claire and I are going. You may stay here with Mother and the little one, if you like; you may bring little Henri back with you to Chantemelle when the bad weather is over.

CLAIRE. I am going with Robert. I — I admire him — so much! [*To Hélène.*] Come Hélène, we have to get ready, and help Robert — Come —

[*Hélène follows Claire out of the room, walking as if she were in a dream.*]

DUKE [*riveted to the floor*]. Robert, I have abdicated! You are the head of the family! Command, they will all obey you! — Good-by! —

[*He picks up his hat and overcoat, and goes out to the beach. The Duchess throws herself into Robert's arms, convulsed with sobs.*]

[CURTAIN.]

ACT IV

[*The same scene as in the first two acts. It is night. The door up-stage to the left*[1] *is open; the passage formed by this door is transformed into a chapel, brightly lighted by candles where the body of Robert is exposed upon a bier.*

The Duchess and Claire are kneeling in prayer before the bier. About them are numerous peasants, men and women, who from time to time cast a glance at the body and pray.

Down-stage to the left sits the Duke, his arms resting on the table, his face buried in his hands. Behind him, near the principal entrance to the room, stands a servant in livery, who conducts the peasants back and forth during the first part of the act.— The peasants go first to the bier, say a "Pater," then cross themselves and go out. Some sprinkle holy water on the body.

For about a minute after the curtain rises, no one speaks.— The visitors enter, then bow ceremoniously to the Duke, who rarely raises his eyes.

A large Farmer, as he leaves the bed, approaches the Duke and offers his condolence.

The Farmer is dressed in his best clothes.]

[1] When the play was produced at the Théâtre Libre, the bier was placed up-stage, center, the head of the body touching the back wall, the feet pointing toward the footlights.— Tr.

THE FARMER. Ah, Monsieur le duc, it's very sad! Such a young man! And so strong! See him galloping away all winter with his dogs! — Maybe he wore himself out doing that? Why, my wife was telling me only this morning, he wasn't afraid of anything, not he! And last Sunday, sick as he was, we saw him at High Mass — and then he went to the cemetery to see the old graves of his ancestors; and he didn't wear a hat — he was there most a quarter of an hour! There was no sense in that! He must 've done it on purpose —

DUKE. This is a terrible blow for me, Renaud — *I* ought to have been the first to go!

THE FARMER. Oh, Monsieur le duc is like a rock yet! — Monsieur Robert used to come around to the farm often — he liked us farmers, and the animals too! He'd 've been a fine master to us later on!

DUKE. We shall do our best to have his son resemble him; he must make the same friends for Chantemelle as his father did!

[*The Duke shakes hands with the Farmer, who goes out.*

After the peasants cease coming in, enter a Neighbor. He wears a fur cap and carries a heavy cane; his thick boots and leather leggings proclaim him a hunter. His trousers and coat are of black cloth. The servant points out the Duke to him.]

THE NEIGHBOR [*going to the Duke*]. My dear friend! [*They shake hands cordially.*] I just heard the sad news this noon. I'd gone out early in the morning shooting wild geese — when

I got back for lunch they told me.— So you didn't arrive soon enough?

DUKE. We arrived just an hour ago.

THE NEIGHBOR. It was over last night, wasn't it?

DUKE. We received the telegram at four in the afternoon.

THE NEIGHBOR. Just in time to catch the train?

DUKE. Yes!

THE NEIGHBOR [*turning toward the body*]. He's there! Poor Robert! I'll go and see him for the last time! I don't like to disturb the ladies; how are they?

DUKE. Tired — utterly worn out —

THE NEIGHBOR. Mademoiselle Claire was here, wasn't she?

DUKE. Yes — she was admirable — my daughter-in-law was here, too.

THE NEIGHBOR. If I can be of any service, I —?

[*The Duke bows his head sadly, shakes hands again with the Neighbor, who goes toward the body. The Duke accompanies him. The Duke is intercepted by a Nun who enters through the door, down-stage to the left. She was Robert's nurse during his last illness.*]

THE NUN. Monsieur le duc, they tell me the village blacksmith is waiting to close the coffin.

DUKE. We've been here hardly an hour! The Duchess wants to keep her son a little longer! Must he —?

THE NUN. Yes!

DUKE. Try to keep the strangers out of the way; I don't want any one by while his mother is with him! You may bring the men in a few moments — afterward!

[*The Duke goes back to his place. The Nun tells the servant to admit no one else, then goes to Claire and whispers something to her, while the servant sends the peasants out. The Neighbor also leaves the room, then the Nun. The Duchess remains at the foot of the bier, oblivious of what is happening. Claire goes to her father, and speaks with him in an undertone.*]

CLAIRE. Father, they are going to close Robert's coffin —! [*Showing him a sheet of paper folded between the leaves of her prayer-book.*] I want to read his will before us all, while he is still with us. Then I shall tell you about his last hours: not the agony, you know about that, but his last wishes. They are worthy of him!

DUKE. You represent your brother: what you wish shall be done.

CLAIRE. Thank you. I am going to call Hélène —

[*She speaks a few words to the servant, who goes out. At the same time the Duchess rises, her face wet with tears, and joins her husband. Claire comes to them.*]

DUCHESS [*looking toward the bier*]. He hasn't changed! He is sleeping!

CLAIRE. He is! He closed his eyes quietly without the least struggle. His last thought was the honor of the family —

DUCHESS. Was Hélène there?

CLAIRE. I called her toward the last.

DUCHESS. Did he recognize her?

CLAIRE. He asked for her.

DUCHESS. Then she didn't go near him all that week while he was sick?

CLAIRE. Oh, yes, she was often with him; we had no reason to send her away. Robert treated her exactly as he had always done — there was only one change in him: he had no desire to live —

DUCHESS [*sobbing*]. His prayer was answered!

CLAIRE. Courage, Mother! You will need a great deal to-day! I have sent for Hélène: I want you all to hear Robert's last wishes —

[*The Duchess again kneels by the bier.*]

DUKE. Your mother can't stand this — how long will she be like that?

CLAIRE. If she can only bear up until the funeral is over!

DUKE. How foolish we were, Claire, to think that with a secret like this we could live together happily! We can stand the strain now, and for some time to come, but — after?

CLAIRE. Then Mother will not suffer so! She loves you too much, she understands her religion too well to leave you.

DUKE. But when I have to face Hélène —

CLAIRE. Hélène will be no obstacle —

DUKE. Is she going to leave? Then she's not going to take the child? I am sure Robert will not allow him to be in unsafe hands. But if Hélène goes away by herself, what will people think?

CLAIRE. Have no fear about that! Hélène

will not leave here alone. The martyrdom you think Mother will have to suffer will be borne by some one else.

DUKE. You, Claire?

CLAIRE [*repressing the tears*]. Please don't ask me! — What I have to look forward to is too terrible to think about. Robert himself will tell you what we are going to do. When you hear the words from his mouth then I shall tell you what is to become of me.

[*Enter Hélène. She stands in the center of the room. The Duke and Claire are down-stage to the right.*]

CLAIRE. Hélène, my mother wishes to see you — there!

[*Hélène goes to the bier. She waits there for the Duchess, who is still on her knees. At last the Duchess rises, and she and Hélène face each other. The Duchess holds her hand out, with her eyes still on the body; Hélène takes her hand for a moment. Then the Duchess goes to Claire and the Duke. They are grouped as follows: the Duke leaning on the table down-stage to the right; the Duchess seats herself to the left, Hélène remains standing before the bier; Claire, standing in the center, reads the will.*]

CLAIRE [*the will in hand*]. Here is Robert's will. The beginning is like those old wills of our forefathers — I can imagine him making a cross for a signature! [*Reading.*]

"In the name of the Father and the Son and the Holy Spirit, I, Robert Charles-Henri de

Chantemelle, about to appear before God, ask pardon for all the wrongs I have committed against my people, and do solemnly swear that I bear in my heart not the slightest resentment against any one of them, whosoever he may be. I wish my father to know that I felt as deeply as he at the thought of the disappearance of our family. He forgot that he was a father only to remember that he was a duke. He had the strength to crush certain sacred sentiments, I to forget vengeance — I thank God for taking my life at a time when such vengeance became impossible for me.

" On my death, I ordain the following:

" I humbly beg my father and my mother to continue their existence together in the true spirit of Christian humility, after I am gone. I have learned a valuable lesson from my mother, which has greatly helped me, and taught me to die in peace.

" Claire has nothing to reproach herself with in regard to me. When at last she saw the impossibility of my surviving she fully realized her responsibility. How willing she is to expiate her noble crime in trying to preserve the ancient glory of our family!

" I should be guilty of grave indelicacy were I to record here what she has promised to do. I leave it to her to explain in what way she is willing to sacrifice herself. Claire will be my representative among you; I place Hélène and her child in Claire's hands. Whatever she shall think best, will be my wish.

" I ask my parents to give to Hélène the

Château des Ecluses in Normandy. She promised me to go there and consecrate her life to the education of her son. She may be justly charged with perjury if she deviates in the slightest degree from this single end. I had the right to demand this oath in return for the forgiveness I granted her." [*Hélène falls to her knees, then to the floor, overcome.*]

" As soon as little Henri shall reach the age of fifteen years, I authorize Hélène to take him to live in Paris for the sake of the superior educational facilities which are to be found only there. The future Duke de Chantemelle must be well educated: the idea that to his rank is to be added personal worth must be inculcated in him. Nothing should be neglected to make him a modern man, in the deepest significance of the word: he must love his country to-day, and understand its glories and its greatness. We shall be lost if we continue to prolong our hates and prejudices, which in the times immediately following the Revolution were quite pardonable, but which nowadays are evidence only of laziness and selfish egotism. The Revolution guillotined our fathers who were at first so ready to sacrifice all for its sake, but *we* use that argument as a pretext to combat every attempt at social betterment. Let us rather carry forward our own traditions by paying for our well-intentioned errors with our lives, and prove thereby that the nobility can at least furnish an object-lesson of self-immolation, and pave the way for the men of our time, too keen of mind, and too forgetful of sentiment! When those who are more unfortunate than we ask for more and better conditions, let us be ready to put ourselves at their head with the idea that those we are leading may fire upon us from behind! The nobility it seems to me has accomplished its ends and is a thing of the past; it has been exploited too much for the sake of wealth, and based too little upon merit: it has ever remained closed to the great men who have sprung from the people, and the people have reciprocated. Before it finally disappears it must by means of a pious lie give the same impression of grandeur of former times that is left by the gigantic fossils which tell us of the greatness of past ages!

"Later, when my heir grows to manhood, I ask that Claire tell him the manner of my death, how his grandparents, his aunt, and his mother, have sacrificed for him, in order that his name should survive without a stain. He must understand that this name, perpetuated by means of a monstrous crime, should be borne with almost superhuman dignity. I want Claire to repeat to him what she said to me yesterday: 'Our lives all end with yours. But what does that matter? We have searched the whole field to find a little flower!'"

DUCHESS [*sobbing*]. Robert!

DUKE. His is the spirit of the race!

CLAIRE. There is something more: about me. I promised Robert never to marry, and to live with Hélène all my life.

DUCHESS. No, no, Claire, not that! To leave me all alone!

CLAIRE [*calmly*]. I made an oath to him! [*Turning toward the bier.*] Robert, again I swear to follow your wife and your son wherever they may go, and help them carry their name with dignity through life. This I consider as a debt of honor contracted in your favor the day I allowed Hélène to enter the family. She and I promise to devote ourselves to the education of the child: to make him first an honest man, and, better, a man capable of dying for the sake of an idea — as you said — and as you did —!

DUCHESS. Claire — good-by! Let me say good-by now: later, I couldn't!

[*Claire throws herself into her mother's arms. They go toward the bier.*]

DUKE [*following them, makes a last prayer by his son, then, after crossing himself, he goes straight to Hélène and looking her in the eyes says in a calm, low voice*]. Good-by — daughter!

[*He goes out.*]

[CURTAIN.]

The Serenade

(*A Bourgeois Study*)

Play in Three Acts

By

JEAN JULLIEN

TRANSLATED BY

BARRETT H. CLARK

Presented for the first time, in Paris, at the Théâtre Libre, December 23, 1887.

To Henry Céard

in grateful recognition
from his confrère

Jean Jullien.

PERSONS REPRESENTED:

THÉODORE COTTIN, *jeweler, 58 years old.*
CALIXTE POUJADE, *Cottin's partner, 45 years old.*
MAXIME CHAMPANET, *25 years old.*
PROSPER POUJADE, *Poujade's nephew, 27 years old.*
DUMOULIN, *52 years old.*
FOURNIER, *servant.*
A CUSTOMER.
NATHALIE COTTIN, *Cottin's wife, 37 years old.*
GENEVIÈVE COTTIN, *Nathalie's daughter, 18 years old.*
CÉLINA ROULARD, *19 years old.*
LÉOCADIE DUMOULIN, *43 years old.*
CLÉMENCE, *18 years old.*
DODO, *Théodore Cottin's son, 9 years old.*
Country neighbors, servants.

The first act takes place in Cottin's jewelry shop, Paris; the second at the Cottins' country house; the third in the Cottins' dining room, Paris.

N.B.— The rôles of Cottin and Poujade should not be assumed by " comic " actors.

The theater should be dark.

THE SERENADE

". . . This revolutionary *Serenade,* which destroyed forever the conventional virginity of ingénues on the stage, and by its happy delineation of the average bourgeois created at once that type of play which has since been termed the Théâtre-Libre play. . . ." (Henry Céard, in *Evènement,* October, 1891.)

ACT I

[*A jeweler's shop in the Palais-Royal.— At the back a glazed door; right, a long table; a door leading to the stair-case; down-stage, a cash desk.— Left, a round table, chairs, and a door behind a portière.— The furniture is severe in style: dark wood with purple plush.*

As the curtain rises, there is still some daylight on the scene.]

POUJADE [*seated before the cash desk, reading a newspaper. Excitedly*]. Another! This *is* too much! — Prosper, did you hear about that crime in the Rue des Vertus?

PROSPER [*at the back, arranging jewel-boxes upon a shelf*]. No, Uncle.

POUJADE. Listen, my boy, and be warned once for all on the comforts of marriage! [*Reading.*] "They had not been living on the best of terms —" Ah! "Last night the neighborhood was aroused by several revolver shots: the husband had just fired upon the guilty pair when the neighbors disarmed him. The lover was killed instantly, the wife died two hours later." What do you say to that, my lover?

PROSPER. I say that there are evil women as well as good; the main point is to choose wisely.

POUJADE. That's exactly where the wisest of us are fooled, my dear Prosper: all women are angels before marriage; afterward they're demons! Of course, I am the first to admit that Cottin's daughter is perfect, adorable; she has — every imaginable good quality; she's intelligent, good-hearted — marry her, and then tell me what you find out.

PROSPER. Uncle, do you think that she —! Mademoiselle Geneviève is —

POUJADE [*authoritatively*]. Let me finish! In the matter of marriage I've had a little more experience than you. I've escaped eleven marriages in my life-time, and I thank God every day for preserving me!

PROSPER. He was wrong to do it!

POUJADE [*going to Prosper*]. But don't you see that some day or other with my quick temper I might have done what that man in the Rue des Vertus did? Bang! I'd have killed every one in the affair and myself into the bargain! [*He shrugs his shoulders and indicates by a gesture the boxes which Prosper has been arranging.*] Another wooden one —?

[*Enter Dumoulin.*]

PROSPER [*runs to him quickly. Smiling*]. Ah, Monsieur Dumoulin!

DUMOULIN [*to Prosper*]. How are you? [*To Poujade, who has advanced from the cash desk and stands holding out his hand.*] How are you, Monsieur Poujade? How is dear old Cottin? And Madame Cottin, and Geneviève, and Dodo; everybody?

POUJADE. Splendid, Monsieur, splendid.

DUMOULIN. Good, good! How is business? Always first-rate? Well, what can you expect, changing parties this way, and with this set of Deputies! Say what you will, as long as they refuse to make commercial laws for merchants, and military laws for soldiers, they'll never get anywhere. Every one to his trade; then the taxpayers are safe! — Ah, the ladies at home told me to ask whether Cottin had decided to go to the country to-morrow?

POUJADE. I'm sure I can't tell you.

PROSPER. It depends on Madame, you know, whether they go or not; if she takes it into her head to stay home, stay home she will.

DUMOULIN [*looking at his watch*]. I'm very busy, and I'd like an answer. Is Cottin here? Can I see him?

POUJADE. He's up-stairs, but he's told me twice he doesn't want to be disturbed. Prosper, go and rap at his door once more.

[*Prosper goes out.*]

DUMOULIN [*maliciously*]. I insist, because the day after to-morrow I've made up my mind to fight a duel with you at La Varenne.

POUJADE. With me?

DUMOULIN [*laughing*]. Yes, you: a duel to death — for the seconds! I want to see which of us, with the same bait, will catch the most fish in two hours! What do you say to that?

POUJADE. Not half bad! You know every corner, every shallow, every pool in the Marne, as well as you do the shelves in your own shop; and you have nicknames for the fish.

DUMOULIN. We'll fish in the same place — I'll follow after you!

POUJADE. Well, the fried fish you'll bring home won't give any one indigestion!

DUMOULIN [*with an air of omniscience*]. We'll see, we'll see whether Normans are as good as Gascons!

PROSPER [*re-entering*]. I rapped and rapped, and Monsieur told me to go to the devil, and Madame said, "All right, all right, Monsieur will be down in two minutes."

DUMOULIN. Hm! Family quarrel! I oughtn't to interfere with a husband when he is so occupied. I'll run along! I know what those things are! Only this morning at my place, I had one; and the reason —! My wife wanted to put on a yellow hat, said it was in style; you should have heard her: "You haven't a grain of taste! You're a tyrant! You never do anything for me! Is there a woman on earth as miserable as I! —" At your service, Monsieur Poujade; keep the duel in mind. Good-by, Prosper. I'll look in again to-morrow.

[*He shakes hands with Prosper, and goes out.*]

POUJADE [*on the threshold*]. Kind regards to the ladies!

[*Poujade and Prosper resume their places as*

before. Footsteps are heard on the stairs. Enter Cottin.]

COTTIN. Well, what is it? What is it you want, Prosper? I have only a moment —

PROSPER. Monsieur Dumoulin was here and wanted to know if you were going to La Varenne to-morrow, and Uncle told me to ask you —

POUJADE [*interrupting*]. Yes, the Dumoulins it seems have organized a little party for Sunday and they want to know if you'd like to go with them.

PROSPER [*going to the door*]. Shall I call him back?

COTTIN. Never mind.— How do I know whether we're going to the country? How can any one decide anything with Nathalie? A fishing party! So you disturb me to tell me about a thing like that? A fishing party with the Dumoulins! If we go, they'll see us: they live next to our villa! — I've been laying down the law to my wife up-stairs for the last hour, and the moment I begin to get the upper hand you break in and spoil everything! Now I've got to start all over again!

POUJADE [*going toward Cottin*]. What's the matter now?

COTTIN [*to Poujade, at the foot of the stairs, as Prosper goes back to his work*]. Nothing new! Same old thing! It's about Dodo! They're filling him so full of education that he won't know anything; they'll kill him! Think of it, a babe of nine reciting fables! You know, Poujade, now he can't even talk! All day at his lessons! Scribbling all the time! And that Monsieur Maxime never leaves him, never does anything but scold his pupil! Are they going to make a professor of the boy? Why on earth should he go into the Technical School if he's going to be a jeweler? And they won't listen to me! I wanted to send him to boarding-school as I did his sister, and keep him there till he was seventeen or eighteen — then there wouldn't have been any question about all this stuff now! Nathalie went into hysterics. No, don't make the child work, he's too delicate! An education at the lycée wasn't good enough — she had a thousand reasons. I had to give in.

POUJADE. And you a man of character! I wouldn't let them pull my nose that way! I'd say "I want!" and I'd be obeyed!

COTTIN. Of course, I don't know anything about education and all that, so I ought to listen to my wife. At bottom, I don't think she's all wrong, but she exaggerates. If I'd had Latin stuffed down my throat all day like Dodo, I'd have gone crazy. Really, I'm worried about him.

POUJADE. Give in to your wife, old man, it's your duty as a husband and father! Struggle with women? Never! [*Confidingly.*] But really, Cottin, now I think of it, you can get rid of one of your tyrants by marrying your daughter.

COTTIN [*shrugging his shoulders*]. You're joking; she's too young anyway, and then you know Geneviève is the dearest creature I have, and I'd like to give her to my dearest friend. You're the man, but unluckily you're a trifle too — old. [*In an undertone.*] Your heir! [*Pointing to Prosper.*]

POUJADE. Not so loud! If he heard you, he'd be sick for joy.

COTTIN [*laughing*]. You think so? So much the better! At least he'll not grow up to be an old curmudgeon, like his uncle!

[*Steps are heard on the stair-case. The voice of a child outside sings*]

VOICE

"On dainty wing the butterfly
Floats from flow'r to flow'r —"

COTTIN. Not so much noise, Monsieur Dodo, please! [*The voice sounds nearer.*] Poor little martyr, must have some fun, I suppose!

[*Cottin sits down near the cash desk. Enter Dodo.*]

DODO. It's me!

[*He crosses the stage with his books under his arm, and makes for the door on the opposite side. He drops some books.*]

COTTIN. Where are you going, you young vagabond?

DODO. There.

COTTIN. What are you going to do?

DODO [*picking up the books*]. Work! Don't I always have to work in this house?

COTTIN. Why there, in the little room?

DODO. Mama told me to.

COTTIN. Another of her ideas! — Weren't you comfortable up-stairs?

DODO. Mama said she wanted to keep an eye on me, and every time she came down to the store she wanted Monsieur Maxime to come down with her!

POUJADE [*who has gone up-stage to Prosper,*

returns to the cash desk]. What do you say to that, Cottin? What have you to complain of?

COTTIN [*with resignation*]. Nothing! [*To Dodo.*] Is your mother coming down soon? She must know I have to go out with Poujade: we have an appointment!

DODO. She'll be down soon.

[*He goes out slowly.*]

COTTIN. I tell you they're killing him! [*He shakes his head lugubriously, then turns round with an air of determination.*] Oh, Poujade, that matter of the diamonds — is it worth bothering about, or shall we let it go?

POUJADE. It's worth considering; if nothing comes of it, we can let it go.

COTTIN [*impatiently; as he rises*]. Why doesn't Nathalie come? [*To Prosper.*] Prosper, go up and tell Madame to hurry. [*Prosper goes out.*] Six o'clock! She'll make us miss that appointment! [*Poujade goes out at the back.*] How tiresome women are, they're never on time! [*Going to the door opening upon the stair-case.*] Nathalie! We're waiting for you, dear!

[*Enter Madame Cottin, followed by Maxime, who carries some articles of clothing on his arm.*]

MME. COTTIN [*sitting at the cash desk*]. Here I am! Here I am! You'd think the house was on fire to hear you shout so!

COTTIN. Did you bring down my hat and coat and umbrella?

[*Poujade is meantime putting on his hat and coat, up-stage.*]

MME. COTTIN. Monsieur Maxime was kind

enough to bring everything: hat, coat, and umbrella.

COTTIN. Why do you trouble Monsieur Maxime? Wasn't Fournier there?

MME. COTTIN. I sent him to do some errands for me.

COTTIN [*hurrying to Maxime who is in the center of the stage*]. I'm very, very sorry, Monsieur Maxime! I don't know why my wife imposes on you so! [*To Mme. Cottin.*] Oh, Nathalie, to think of Monsieur Maxime's carrying my things!

MAXIME. Nonsense, Monsieur Cottin, I'm only too glad to be of service to you!

COTTIN [*relieving Maxime of the clothes*]. I hear they've changed your working quarters in the house; they've put you in the customers' waiting room.

MAXIME [*passing to the left of Cottin, and helping him put on his coat*]. Yes, Madame thought the room we had been using was too much exposed to the brightness of the setting sun, that it would be too hot in the evenings.

COTTIN [*interrupting*]. What, Dodo's room exposed to the setting sun?

MME. COTTIN [*aside to her husband*]. I told him that as an excuse; I merely want to keep watch.

COTTIN [*aside*]. That's wise. [*Aloud.*] Yes, I think you'll be more comfortable down here. [*To Poujade.*] Are you ready, Poujade? [*To Mme. Cottin.*] That bill from Durandeau will probably come; pay it. Then there's that insurance agent's watch to be fixed.— Send for Madame de Champtonnerre's necklace. That's all, I think.

Sell as many chronometers as possible: they're not worth a sou nowadays. [*He starts to go, but comes back.*] Excuse me, dear, I almost forgot! [*He kisses her.*]

MME. COTTIN. I forgive you. [*She kisses him. Cottin and Poujade go out.*]

MME. COTTIN [*going toward Maxime, who stands apart*]. One for him; two for you!

[*She kisses him on both cheeks.*]

MAXIME. You must be careful. What if he had forgotten his handkerchief, or his cane — or anything?

MME. COTTIN. Love doesn't think of such things, Maxime. [*She brings him down to the cash desk, and makes him sit by her side.*] Here, sit next to me — close. I want to see you, hear you, look at you — my poet! Repeat to me again some of those beautiful and graceful words that carry me up into the clouds; recite those love verses you whispered to me the other evening: about Spring, and the honeysuckles and the flowers —

MAXIME [*sulkily*]. What put it into your head to have me give my lessons here? Weren't we much better in the other room? Any one might find us here, a customer, a shop-keeper —

DODO [*entering*]. M'sieu! — M'sieu! I've copied the paragraph. What must I copy now?

MME. COTTIN. Dodo, you're awful; can't you be good for two minutes? You're very naughty! When I'm talking with your teacher, I don't want to be interrupted. Copy the next paragraph and don't disturb us!

DODO. I've finished the chapter — I can't copy the next paragraph.

MME. COTTIN. Begin with the next chapter.

MAXIME [*rising*]. I'll show him — he can't find the place.

MME. COTTIN [*retaining Maxime*]. Don't go, he's old enough to find out for himself.

MAXIME. Do what your mother tells you: begin the next chapter. I'll come and see how you're getting on in a minute.

[*Dodo goes out.*]

MME. COTTIN [*to Maxime, severely*]. Now, Monsieur, tell me what debauches you had last night; where did you go?

MAXIME. A number of us met and had our monthly dinner — there was music, and we recited poetry.

MME. COTTIN. Did you recite?

[*Dodo, who had slowly made his retreat comes back laughing.*]

DODO. There aren't any more chapters!

MME. COTTIN [*very angry*]. Back again, Dodo!? You're going to take your note-book, Monsieur, and write out twice the whole conjugation, "I am a disobedient and rude boy."

DODO. Well, I can't help it if the book stops!

[*He goes out, with tears in his eyes.*]

MME. COTTIN. What *did* you recite?

MAXIME. *The Serenade.*

MME. COTTIN. Oh, *The Serenade!* How they must have applauded! Did they call you back twenty times and carry you around in triumph!? Oh, what a lovely poem it is! So full of love! And you recite it so passionately! I'll never forget the night I heard it for the first time! Do you remember, Maxime?

MAXIME. Oh, I've repeated it so often —!

MME. COTTIN [*in the clouds*]. It was a Sunday; we were in the country, at La Varenne, with the Dumoulins and our cousins the Boulards. It was night, we were on the terrace — a hot night, and the air was full of perfume! I never had such a lovely sensation! Your voice rippled like a nightingale's — I was yours then, you had completely conquered me! Don't you remember, afterwards, among the young vines, the kisses —

MAXIME [*coldly*]. Oh, so that was the day?

MME. COTTIN. And the Boulards and the Dumoulins who were looking everywhere for us! What if they had found us!

MAXIME. I can't imagine what led you — why, only a few steps away from your husband!

MME COTTIN. Can you think of such things at a time like that? Think how careful we've had to be since! To avoid any suspicion!

MAXIME. Are you sure your husband suspects nothing?

MME. COTTIN. Do you think he would act this way if he did?

MAXIME. No, but I think I see him hiding something under his good-natured appearance. Take care, he may be spying! The way he gives in to everything you ask — it may be a trap. I'd feel sorry for you if he ever found out!

MME. COTTIN. I know he's a thousand miles from suspecting anything. He thinks you are very much interested in Dodo's education. In case he heard or thought he saw anything suspicious, I should simply deny everything, and he'd believe me.

MAXIME. But how about Poujade?

MME. COTTIN. He's more blind than my husband! And blindness in an old bachelor is the worst of all! Poujade! He'd swallow any story you gave him. He's easier to deceive with his fierce look than Cottin with his appearance of kindness. Cottin knows women, but he doesn't know Woman!

MAXIME. And his nephew?

MME. COTTIN. Hm! Ssh! [*Aside*]. Speak of the devil —

[*Enter Prosper, back. He looks for something in one of the show-cases.*]

[*Aloud to Maxime*]. Then you don't think a whole chapter is too much to learn, Monsieur? Please don't tire him out: his health isn't too good, you know!

MAXIME. I shall follow your wishes, Madame.

[*He goes out, left.*]

PROSPER [*with a jewel-box in his hand*]. Madame, I have looked everywhere, but I can't find Fournier.

MME. COTTIN. That's not strange. If you'd asked me I could have told you: I sent him on some errands. What did you want him for?

PROSPER. To go to the shop and get Madame de Champtonnerre's necklace.

MME. COTTIN. That's too bad! You'd better go to the shop yourself and get it.

PROSPER [*hesitating a moment*]. That would be the easiest way; I'll go at once.

[*Prosper goes out. Mme. Cottin leaves the cash desk and goes to the door, left, making a sign to Maxime.*]

[*Re-enter Maxime.*]

MME. COTTIN. One word more, Monsieur Maxime! [*She drops the portière over the door.*] Leave him to write out his conjugation, and come and talk with me. We have so little time together! [*They sit down on chairs, next each other.*]

MAXIME [*ill at ease*]. So you think this Monsieur Prosper, who looks daggers at me all the time, hasn't the least suspicion? Do you think he hasn't heard by chance some of our foolish conversations, some stray word?

MME. COTTIN [*laughing*]. No! And the reason is so simple that I wonder you haven't seen it! Do you know why Poujade's nephew is working in our shop?

MAXIME. To learn the trade, isn't he?

MME. COTTIN. There's another reason.

MAXIME. Perhaps his uncle hopes he'll succeed him some day?

MME. COTTIN. Come, you can guess; it's not so hard. Poujade has a nephew, my husband has a daughter; they are about the same age —

MAXIME [*rising*]. He marry Geneviève!?

MME. COTTIN. Why not?

MAXIME [*taking his chair to the table*]. Of course — why — not?

MME. COTTIN [*also rising*]. Now do you see why Prosper can't suspect us? He is very much in love with Geneviève —

MAXIME. Are you sure of that?

MME. COTTIN. Absolutely sure. If he does look daggers at you, it's only because he thinks you are trying to please me for another reason;

he believes you are a rival, that you're making love to his sweetheart. Amusing, isn't it?

MAXIME. Do you imagine that he thinks I'm in love with Mademoiselle Geneviève?

MME. COTTIN. I'm sure of it, and furthermore I'll do my best to keep him thinking so. The other evening, when I was talking with the Boulards, I gave him to understand that you had asked for Nini's hand in marriage, and that you had not been refused. He was simply furious, and left the room without saying a word! How I laughed!

MAXIME [*troubled*]. You were wrong to do that; see what an awkward position you put me in. If you make it appear that I want to marry Mademoiselle Geneviève, then I'll have to act the part, and pretend to —

MME. COTTIN. So much the better. We'll have so many more chances for meeting! It's so much nicer to see you here than in that hotel where we used to meet.

MAXIME. But I'm in a nice fix with Mademoiselle Geneviève! How can I make love to her without asking her to marry me? I'm not very good at being sentimental, and my platonic love —!! What will she say? What will she think of a lover who draws back the moment he ought to propose? I'll have to act a perfect cad!

MME. COTTIN. She won't object; you don't know how simple these boarding-school girls are. They don't know the A, B, C of love. I really don't think you would stand the slightest chance with her anyway. No offense?

MAXIME. The idea!

48273

MME. COTTIN. Oh, your lordship, she has made her choice already. Prosper is the man, and I don't think it's a half-bad match. They're not too much in love, and both will make excellent shop-keepers. She may change some day, maybe she'll find *her* Maxime! Come here, kiss me! [*She kisses him, then resumes her place at the cash desk, Maxime following her.*] You haven't yet told me how your evening ended?

MAXIME. It was late — the night was a bit chilly, so I went straight home, in company with the stars of night, and went to bed.

MME. COTTIN. There were women at the banquet, weren't there? Actresses — mm — women — ?

MAXIME. No — really — not a single one.

MME. COTTIN. Not one? You're lying, there were, I can see it in your eyes! Don't try to deny it!

MAXIME. My dear Nathalie, I tell you —

[*A customer enters, after having examined at some length the goods exhibited in the windows.*]

CUSTOMER [*to Maxime*]. Monsieur, I've seen your big advertisements in the papers; chronometers for twelve francs — guaranteed for two years. May I see one?

MME. COTTIN [*without moving or even turning her head*]. Monsieur, we haven't any just now; we'll have some to-morrow. Come back then, will you?

CUSTOMER. Well, you have those eighteen-franc chronometers, at any rate? I see some over there!

MME. COTTIN [*as before*]. Yes, but they're not guaranteed, I don't advise you to buy one of those.

CUSTOMER. Well, how about the twenty-franc ones?

MME. COTTIN [*immovable*]. They're not reliable.

CUSTOMER. I'll come back later, then.

[*He goes out.*]

MME. COTTIN [*rises and goes to the center of the stage, looking at the door*]. To think that I was born to be a jeweler's wife! Argue with customers, listen to their complaints, haggle over a sou, or the price of a watch! I was never understood! No one ever really understands me! My heart is bursting! Oh, Maxime, Maxime, you don't love me, you have stopped loving me! You were with those women last night — I know you were!

MAXIME. But I tell you I wasn't! I repeat —!

MME. COTTIN. You're moody, Maxime, you've been like that the past few days, you hardly say a word, you're not the way you used to be, during the first days. You don't talk the way you did then! You seem afraid to be near me! Do you — do you feel guilty?

MAXIME [*coldly and without showing any enthusiasm*]. How ridiculous! Nothing of the kind! I've never been so happy in my life! Haven't I everything I could wish for? To be near you?!

MME. COTTIN. No, you're changed! Before, you'd have kissed me twenty times while you were saying that! Maxime, I have a rival! I feel it! Oh, I'm so miserable!

[*She falls on a chair near the table.*]

MAXIME. Really, Nathalie, your jealousy is ridiculous; you're not at all the same woman you were; this is all nonsense. Do you imagine that when I have you I can think of anything else? Would I leave you? If I seem a little — out of sorts to-day — it's because I have a headache. I must have had a little too much champagne last night.

MME. COTTIN [*going to him*]. And you wouldn't tell me you were sick! Poor dear!

MAXIME. It's only a simple headache. To-morrow I'll be quite well.

MME. COTTIN. It's more than a simple headache; you have a fever! Have some mint; I'll get you some! Or some brandy! Or a glass of Madeira! I'll get ready some tea for you!

[*She runs to the door, right.*]

MAXIME. No, please don't! Nathalie, please!

MME. COTTIN. Drink the tea; or I won't believe a word of what you've said!

[*The door-bell rings; enter Geneviève, followed by a maid carrying a roll of music.*]

GENEVIÈVE [*comes in smiling at her mother*]. Hello, Mama? [*To Maxime.*] How are you, Monsieur? [*Maxime bows.*] Mademoiselle says I've never been in such good voice as to-day. I sang my big number three times; she was delighted. She complimented me and said what a pity it was I couldn't go on the stage!

MME. COTTIN [*not interested*]. Singing

teachers always say that! [*To the maid, as she goes out.*] Marie, make the tea at once for Monsieur Maxime, please.

GENEVIÈVE [*to Maxime, who is near the table*]. Sick, Monsieur Maxime?

MAXIME. Your mother is too kind; it's merely a headache. It's nothing at all!

MME. COTTIN. Merely a headache that makes him sad, out of sorts — Don't try to hide it, Monsieur Maxime: you're sick, very sick. Isn't he, Geneviève?

GENEVIÈVE. That's so. How pale you are!

MAXIME [*laughing*]. I have no time for sickness!

[*Enter Cottin and Poujade.*

Geneviève runs and kisses her father, then returns to talk with Maxime].

MME. COTTIN. Back again? [*To Poujade.*] How about the diamonds?

POUJADE. Ask Cottin.

COTTIN [*going to the cash desk and arranging the papers*]. No, you tell her!

POUJADE [*center*]. Well, Madame, a fresh triumph for your husband!

COTTIN [*shrugging his shoulders*]. You always put it that way! I have nothing to do with it, it's merely the House of Cottin-Poujade.

MME. COTTIN. Tell us, Poujade.

POUJADE [*advancing*]. The moment the other bidders saw Cottin, they retired from the field! The whole thing was over in two seconds; when he offered to give references, they made fun of him: "Cottin, a man like M. Cottin, known through all the business world of Paris for more than thirty years for his financial integrity, a man held in high esteem, a man to whom everybody would like to be a debtor! Ask references from Monsieur Cottin? It would be a disgrace to ask for it!"

COTTIN. Why, Poujade, they spoke of the House, not me!

POUJADE [*going up-stage*]. House if you like, but yours was the credit, you are the most important part of the House!

COTTIN. No one can be in business as long as I have and not get to be well known. There's no need exaggerating!

POUJADE [*turns round and sees Madame Cottin crossing the stage with a cup of tisane,*[1] *which she has just received from the maid*]. Hello, who's this tisane for? Is someone sick?

GENEVIÈVE. Yes — Monsieur Maxime. Didn't you notice how badly he was looking?

POUJADE. Why, what's the matter, Professor, indigestion of Latin, or did you get choked on Philosophy?

COTTIN [*rising quickly from his chair*]. Monsieur Maxime sick? My dear Monsieur!

MAXIME [*coming forward*]. Nothing, Messieurs, only a slight headache. I have them from time to time —

COTTIN. You'd better go home and to bed; that's the best thing to do.

POUJADE [*at the back*]. Drink a big glass of punch, hire a nurse, and sweat the whole thing out of your system!

[1] A light hot drink, usually flavored with orange.

MME. COTTIN [*eagerly*]. You'd better go home, Monsieur Maxime! Take my advice, don't try to give your lesson this evening.

GENEVIÈVE [*giving him the cup of tisane*]. Drink it down boiling hot.

MAXIME. I'll burn my mouth!

POUJADE. What's the difference? Drink it, man!

MME. COTTIN [*calling through the door, right*]. Fournier, Monsieur Maxime's hat and coat, at once!

COTTIN [*taking Maxime's hand*]. You have a fearful fever, don't take cold now. The weather's changing, and you might easily come down with bronchitis — and you can't fool with bronchitis!

POUJADE [*shrugging his shoulders*]. I know how to treat bronchitis: a dozen punches!

[*Enter Fournier with Maxime's coat and hat. Mme. Cottin and Geneviève help him put on the coat.*]

MME. COTTIN. There!

GENEVIÈVE [*turning up his collar*]. Keep your neck covered.

MME. COTTIN. Yes, take care of your throat!

MAXIME. Ladies, I'm quite embarrassed; I can't tell you —

MME. COTTIN. Don't speak of it! Fournier, you go with Monsieur Maxime to his rooms.

[*Fournier bows.*]

COTTIN. That's right, run along. If you don't feel well enough, don't come to-morrow; take a rest. Good-night!

[*Enter Dodo, having just heard the last words.*]

DODO.

> " Vacation at last!
> Our troubles are past!
> Our teachers and books
> In the fire we cast!"

MME. COTTIN. Heartless little wretch! What if he were to be very sick?

GENEVIÈVE. Yes, what if your teacher were to have an awful fever?

COTTIN [*simply*]. No, I think it'll be bronchitis if anything; I'll tell you why: bronchitis is a disease of the vocal organs, and the vocal organs are connected with the brain; that always begins with a headache!

POUJADE [*laughing*]. I'll tell you what's the matter with him! I'll bet he had a high old time last night, and wants to rest up for to-night again!

MME. COTTIN. Poujade, to say that about Monsieur Maxime!

POUJADE. There's nothing wrong in that! Boys will be boys! It's only natural. You needn't worry!

COTTIN [*looking at his watch*]. Hurry up, dinner's ready, children, let's not keep the cook waiting.

[*He goes toward the stairs.*]

MME. COTTIN [*stays down-stage with Geneviève. Poujade lights the gas at the back.*] Perhaps Poujade is right? What if it were only a pretext?

GENEVIÈVE. Oh, Mama, wouldn't he have told the truth?

MME. COTTIN. I'll soon know. [*Aside, in an undertone.*] Then you'll have me to deal with, Monsieur Maxime!

[CURTAIN.]

ACT II

[The terrace of a country house. Right, a porch and a garden; down-stage, a table and chairs. Left, the entrance to the house; the lighted windows of the drawing-room are seen from an angle.— A group of young girls and young men are playing and conversing together.

It is night, and the trees are festooned with lanterns; a large lantern is on the table; this lights up the flower garden.

Madame Cottin, Geneviève, Madame Dumoulin, Célina Boulard, Clémence, are seated in a circle; Maxime, Prosper, and the other young people stand behind the rest.]

MAXIME [*to Célina*]. Here's my basket; What do I get?

CÉLINA. Hm! Charming young man!

GENEVIÈVE. Forfeit! forfeit! That's the third time it's been said! Try something else, Célina.

CÉLINA. What do you want me to say?

MAXIME. Nothing else, Mademoiselle, please! What you have already said is too flattering to have you take it back. [*To Geneviève.*] I give the forfeit to Mademoiselle Célina.

CÉLINA [*to Prosper*]. I pass the basket to you, Monsieur Prosper; what do I get?

PROSPER [*glancing at Maxime*]. One pawn!

MAXIME [*turning to Prosper*]. A fool!

PROSPER. They go together!

MAXIME [*going up to Prosper*]. I think a little breeding would do you no harm!

PROSPER. And for yourself, a little less — arrogance!

MME. COTTIN. Now, Messieurs, what is the matter? Is this the way you play at innocent games? Monsieur Maxime, Prosper, please, please: we're all friends here — no quarrels, please!

MAXIME. Madame, your request is too reasonable for me to refuse. [*To Prosper.*] I shall be happy to discuss the matter with you later. [*He resumes his place behind Mme. Cottin.*]

GENEVIÈVE. Messieurs, that wasn't at all nice of you — to spoil our game. We don't know now where we were — it's as bad as if we were playing Rhymes.

CLÉMENCE. Oh, I'm tired of Charades, and Rhymes, and Puns!

MME. COTTIN. Maybe Monsieur Maxime would be good enough to recite something?

GENEVIÈVE AND CÉLINA. Oh yes, Monsieur Maxime!

MAXIME [*maliciously*]. Oh, not first! After Monsieur! [*Indicating Prosper.*]

PROSPER. As you please!

[*He comes forward within the circle and turns to Geneviève.*]

"TRIOLET TO THE GIRL I LOVE:"

"In the pleasant season of love —"

[*Enter Poujade and Dumoulin, followed by Cottin. They come down-stage conversing, while Cottin stops near the table.*]

POUJADE. You saw the pear they left! Well, the ones they took were twice as big!

DUMOULIN [*stopping*]. You don't mean it!

POUJADE. Twice as big? No, some of them were three times as big! If I'd caught them stealing those pears, I'd give 'em a piece of my mind!

DUMOULIN [*continues walking again*]. Yes, I know you! You wouldn't have left enough to recognize!

THE COMPANY. Ssh! Ssh!

GENEVIÈVE. Silence, Messieurs! There's a recitation going on!

POUJADE. Suppose we've got to listen!

DUMOULIN. Let's hear it!

[*Cottin sits by the small table, right; he leans his elbows upon it. Dumoulin and Poujade stand at the opposite side of the stage.*]

PROSPER [*reciting in an awkward manner*].

"TRIOLET TO THE GIRL I LOVE."

" Love's happy hour at last is come,
And through the forest sweetly sound
The songs of birds in harmony —
Love's happy hour at last is come!
My love then from her cottage comes
She's charming as she minuets
And nods and am'rously coquets —
My love then from her cottage comes.

[*With a threatening glance at Maxime.*]

"Two strutting cocks her favors court
And by her side their feathers preen;
One timid, one the other sort —
Two strutting cocks her favors court.
First one in tender strains holds forth,
The other sings a Serenade —
Two strutting cocks her favors court
And by her side their feathers preen.
[*In despair.*]

"The foolish cock, with hand on breast
Awaits the other's fond advance:
'Cocorico!'— he tries his best,
The foolish cock with hand on breast!
He wins her, takes her far away,
Their quarrel ended that fair day:
The foolish cock with hand on breast —
The other killed himself —'twas best!" [1]
[*He sits down, overcome.*]

CÉLINA. Bravo, Monsieur Prosper! That's lovely! You're a poet, too!

POUJADE. Very nice, but too many repetitions for me. Where did you come across that rigmarole?

DUMOULIN. An Apologue, isn't it, Monsieur Prosper? Who wrote it?

MAXIME [*answering for Prosper*]. An author who knows no more of the laws of prosody than of courtesy.

MME. COTTIN. Your turn, Monsieur Maxime!

[1] As the original is hardly poetic and, as Maxime says, not in accordance with the laws of prosody, an approximation only is attempted in the English rendering.— TR.

[*Poujade and Dumoulin go up-stage, and return by way of the table by which Cottin is sitting.*]

GENEVIÈVE. Oh, yes, Monsieur Maxime!

MAXIME. I don't know a thing about such learned matters!

MME. COTTIN. Come now, recite the *Serenade* for us!

GENEVIÈVE. Yes, the *Serenade,* the *Serenade!*

MAXIME. Not that, it's too trivial.

GENEVIÈVE. No, we want the *Serenade!*

MAXIME [*advancing*]. *The Serenade:*

COTTIN [*rising*]. I agree with Monsieur Champanet; let's have something else.

GENEVIÈVE. Why not? It's so sweet and lovely! Yes, the *Serenade!*

COTTIN. Too sweet and lovely for these young people. When young girls are present, we should choose more modest subjects!

GENEVIÈVE. Papa, you're wrong, the *Serenade* —

COTTIN [*severely*]. I am not mistaken! I tell you once for all I don't intend to have any such filth around here! In the presence of my children!

[*The ladies rise.*]

MME. DUMOULIN [*to Mme. Cottin*]. My dear, what is the matter with your husband today? He is touchy!

MME. COTTIN [*center*]. Some marauders have made him angry, I suppose. [*Speaking to the young people.*] Since you are not allowed to recite, children, you'd better go into the drawing-room; there you may sing and dance as much as you like!

[*The young men offer their arms to the ladies. Mme. de Cottin chooses Maxime ostentatiously; she speaks to him in a confiding way, and once she kisses him. Cottin, who sees this, rises, goes a little way toward them, then returns to his place and sits down.*]

DUMOULIN [*continuing his conversation with Poujade*]. Then you use only white bait?

POUJADE. If you'll come down to my part of the country, I'll show you how to fish!

DUMOULIN. Yes, I know, in the Midi it's easy — more fish than water, as you say — but, tell me this, did any one ever catch a fifteen-pound pike in your country? Well, I did, Monsieur, and Boulard, who's here to-night, can tell you whether I'm telling the truth or not — so can Cottin.

COTTIN [*troubled*]. Yes, yes, that pike of yours was fully fifteen pounds.

DUMOULIN. It was just before I got to Nogent: I was sitting under the willows, fishing with a long line. All at once I saw an enormous fish, a female full of eggs; it darted from under the bank. I said to myself, "Dumoulin, you'll never get her!" I saw her trick, then I had an idea — my heart was thumping at a great rate — instinct, Monsieur Poujade, instinct, it was! — Well, I took my net, got down flat on my stomach —

POUJADE. That's not *fishing!*

DUMOULIN. Wait a moment! Whoop-la! I plunge the net into the water in the twinkling of an eye and hold it hard against the bank — I got the pike! But that wasn't the end: I had to haul it up the side — it was mighty high — ask Monsieur Cottin, he knows how high it was!

COTTIN [*more and more troubled*]. What was high?

DUMOULIN. The bank where I caught the pike.

COTTIN. Still talking about that pike?

DUMOULIN. Then I took hold of the iron frame of the net, and leaned over as far as I could without falling, and brought it slowly toward me. Half-way up I almost lost the fish — nearly fell myself, too! — then I haul again, and there's the fish lying on the bank! I threw my coat over it, rolled it up, and ran home with it. Fifteen pounds it weighed! Cottin was there, he can tell you if I'm lying!

COTTIN. That pike, yes: fifteen pounds.

POUJADE. I know one better than that: a man in our part of the country —

[*Madame Dumoulin appears on the porch.*]

MME. DUMOULIN. Dumoulin, Dumoulin!

DUMOULIN. One minute, Léocadie, we're talking important business!

MME. DUMOULIN [*approaching them*]. We need you for the Quadrille.

DUMOULIN. I don't know how to dance!

MME. DUMOULIN. No matter; you can learn, it's not hard.

DUMOULIN [*rising*]. I've got to go, or she'll never give me a moment's peace. You can tell me your story afterward.

[*He goes out.*]

[*During the following conversation, the piano accompaniment to the Quadrille is heard.*]

POUJADE [*to Cottin, who walks back and forth*]. I can't make you out, Cottin! No use getting mad about one poor little pear you had stolen from you, and looking out of sorts all day long! Are you afraid they'll steal something else? Poujade is here, and I'll tell you, if one of them comes in my direction it'll be the last time!

COTTIN. You're a great one to talk, Poujade!

POUJADE [*sarcastically*]. I notice that when you're in a bad humor you seem mighty big and mighty — the way you were just now. What's the use, now? It's not worth while.

COTTIN. Not worth while? The things they did before my daughter!

POUJADE [*rising*]. He's said the same things twenty times before you!

COTTIN. That may be; perhaps he did use to — that's not to-day!

POUJADE. What about to-day, old man?

COTTIN [*taking Poujade's arm*]. To-day, Poujade, things are happening in my family that are — terrible! There's an awful comedy being played right under my roof — I've seen it with my own eyes. The thieves I want to get hold of are not the ones around the garden; they can steal as many pears as they like, I don't care a snap! *They* [*indicating the drawing-room*] are the ones I'm after! You said I seemed mighty big and strong; well, I'm only beginning: I'm going to see this thing through —!

POUJADE. What? Who?

COTTIN. Monsieur Champanet! Haven't you noticed anything, Poujade?

POUJADE [*evasively*]. Nothing! Well, that is, you'd have to be blind not to. For that matter, your wife doesn't try to hide anything; she might just as well tell everybody!

COTTIN [*bursting out*]. How she could have the audacity, the —

POUJADE. What audacity is there in saying that Monsieur Champanet is in love with Geneviève? What if he does make love to her — so long as he intends to marry her? It's plain enough that's what he wants to do. Ask Prosper what he thinks of it all?

COTTIN. What? Does my wife say that? That's outrageous! It's only a trick to hide something else!

POUJADE [*laughing*]. The idea! You are in a bad humor! You'll kill the lot of us without turning a hair!

COTTIN [*confidingly*]. I say, Poujade, that Champanet is Nathalie's lover! Now do you understand?

POUJADE [*smiling*]. Another of your ideas! You're jealous!

COTTIN. You fool, I know it! I'm sure! Didn't you see them kiss just now? Right in front of us!

POUJADE [*surprised*]. Nonsense!

COTTIN. I was already suspicious; I noticed little signs between them, a word or two now and then — I was on the lookout. That gentleman has always been a little too nice; he's taking too much interest in Dodo's education! I began to have doubts. I kept my eyes open to-night without saying anything. Now I have sure proof.

POUJADE. You're making too much of this, Cottin; you're too jealous — you only want to make sure of what you suspect. Why didn't you ever suspect me of being in love with your wife?

COTTIN. No, Poujade, you're an honorable man; I'd never think that of you. But that damned peacock, with his fine conversation, I tell you, I'm sure about him. I've seen!

POUJADE [*seriously*]. Then you ought to have killed him!

COTTIN [*shrugging his shoulders*]. There you are all over again! Kill him! You don't kill a man like that, right off! I'm not a soldier; have I got the weapons?

POUJADE [*walking away from Cottin*]. Kill him any way! Use your feet, your fists — knock him over the head with a club! Good God! [*Coming back to Cottin.*] What are you going to do?

COTTIN. I'm going to tell him — what a low trick he's done, and then — well, I won't allow him around on any pretext. And if I find him with my wife again —

POUJADE. Well?

COTTIN [*gravely*]. He'll have me to deal with!

POUJADE. That may do for him, but how about your wife —?

COTTIN [*hesitating*]. She — that's a hard question; I want to punish her in a way she won't soon forget.

POUJADE [*firmly*]. Kill her.

COTTIN. Poujade, how can you say that? Think!

POUJADE [*returning, sits by the table*]. The moment you talk of extreme measures — why, that's the only thing to do! If you're too weak to do that, divorce her, old man, or else —

COTTIN [*rising*]. Why, I can't do that! Think of the scandal, and the talk! It would ruin the business, not to mention — [*He sits down again on the chair, center.*]

[*Maxime appears on the porch, cooling himself after the dance. He goes toward the table where Cottin and Poujade are conversing.*]

MAXIME. Messieurs, the ladies have asked me to tell you that they are starting a game where all will be needed; they want you to come in and be banker.

POUJADE [*aside to Cottin*]. Be a man now; this is your chance!

COTTIN [*aside, turning his back to Maxime*]. Not now: later!

POUJADE [*aside to Cottin*]. No, now! It's high time!

MAXIME. What shall I tell the ladies?

POUJADE. They're in no hurry. Sit down a little while here: Cottin has a few words to say to you.

MAXIME. At your service. [*He sits down.*]

POUJADE. He would like to ask you a question. A friend of ours has had trouble in his family — he learned that his wife had a lover.

COTTIN [*aside to Poujade*]. Oh, Poujade, not now!

POUJADE [*aside to Cottin*]. Leave it to me!

[*To Maxime.*] Our friend learned the truth, and now he wants to punish his wife and the lover very severely. You are a man of experience; how was adultery punished in ancient times?

COTTIN [*aside to Poujade*]. There you are, using strong words!

MAXIME. Well, they were primitive enough in those days; sometimes the victims were drawn and quartered; some were drowned, some bound to the tails of horses, others were stripped and left to die out-of-doors. The punishments varied according to the development of civilization. Our civilization, for instance, takes the attitude that in the majority of cases the husband is to blame; the erring wife is nearly always forgiven. [*Cottin rises, and walks about up-stage.*] Before advising your friend, I must know something about him, and find out how much he is to blame.

POUJADE. So you don't admit that the husband has a right to kill the lover?

MAXIME. Never! In good everyday French that is called murder. You must judge these things not according to the anger of the husband; furthermore, you can't do justice yourself in these cases!

COTTIN [*who has slowly advanced toward Maxime*]. I see, Monsieur Champanet, that you advise mercy; I agree with you. My reasons are not the same as yours, but I think we agree at bottom.

POUJADE [*aside to Cottin*]. Go on, give it to him!

COTTIN. Monsieur, this evening as I was in the hallway up-stairs, I saw a man come out of my wife's room.

POUJADE [*aside to Cottin*]. Go on!

COTTIN. That man of course was you: my son's tutor, a friend of my family, a man in whom I had the greatest confidence!

MAXIME [*rising*]. Why, Monsieur Cottin, I don't see the joke! You think me capable —?

COTTIN. I saw you, Monsieur. Even if a man is cowardly enough to deceive and outrage a man, he ought at least to have courage enough to take the responsibility for what he has done!

POUJADE [*aside to Cottin*]. Bravo, Cottin!

MAXIME. Now, Monsieur Cottin, let me —

COTTIN. No, Monsieur, no explanations! You are my wife's lover! Deny it if you dare!

[*Maxime retreats, bowing.*]

POUJADE [*rising with clenched fists*]. Oh, if I only —!

MAXIME. Very well, Monsieur — I — I acknowledge it: I've abused your confidence, your friendship — my life is at your disposal —

COTTIN. What shall I do about it?

MAXIME. Whatever you like. Only listen to me first!

COTTIN [*quivering with anger*]. No, Monsieur, I don't want to hear another word from you; you've lost the right to speak in the house that you've dishonored. I don't want to hear you, or see you; your damned fine words and your open honest face — they're all lies! So you make me a present of your life! Fine compensation, isn't it, for taking away what was dearest in the world to me!?

[*Dodo appears on the porch, and shouts:*]

DODO. Papa, Monsieur Poujade, Monsieur

Maxime; Mama wants to know if you'll be much longer? Everything's all ready; they're waiting for you!

COTTIN [*between his teeth*]. I only want to hear that you were for a moment carried away — you didn't know what you were doing — that, that the whole affair only lasted a short while!

DODO [*stamping with his feet*]. Papa, they're waiting! Come right now!

[*Dodo skips back indoors.*]

COTTIN [*seriously*]. His life! If I took it would I be any better off? Could I ever forget what I have suffered this past week? And after this night? You can't understand what I feel in a case like this; I've been honest and upright in my business all my life, and now to have my wife — I believed her so good, so pure! — the mother of my children — and this blackguard! To think that my wife, whom I have respected and loved for twenty years, is no better than a woman of the streets!

[*He falls into a chair.*]

POUJADE. Come, come, Cottin, courage! You need it now more than ever!

[*Mme. Cottin descends the stairs from the porch, and goes quickly to Cottin.*]

MME. COTTIN. Oh, you men! What's the matter? Afraid of thieves again?

MAXIME [*aside to Mme. Cottin*]. Madame, Monsieur Cottin knows everything!

MME. COTTIN [*aside to Maxime*]. You told him! I thought you were more of a man! You're a fool!

MAXIME [*to Mme. Cottin*]. He saw us.

MME. COTTIN [*to Maxime*]. Deny it anyway!

POUJADE [*hesitatingly, to Cottin*]. You've begun now, Cottin, better get it over with at once!

COTTIN [*solemnly*]. Madame, eighteen years ago, when I married you, you were a young girl who had to work hard for a living; you lived with your mother in a little room in the Rue Vielle-du-Temple. You were well educated, that's true, better than girls of your position usually are, but on my side —

MME. COTTIN [*impatiently*]. Yes, yes, come to the point!

COTTIN. The point is this, Madame: in return for my kindness, my love for you, my confidence in you, you have deceived me, you have forgotten your duties as wife, as the mother of my children and —

MME. COTTIN. Continue, dear, you're getting very interesting. You might think we were at the Ambigu.[2] There's nothing funnier than to see a serious and reasonable man talking the way you are now.

COTTIN. Stop it! I'll have no more of your impudence! I'm not myself, I tell you — just now!

MME. COTTIN [*sarcastically*]. You! Nonsense! When did you change? Now, Théodore, dear little Théodore, don't use strong language and don't get angry. Don't you see that people have been playing a joke on you, telling this absurd story? They've fooled you, because you're a big jealous boy! Ask Poujade!

[2] A famous theater where melodramas used to be performed.

COTTIN [*very excitedly*]. You're no better than a prostitute!

MME. COTTIN. Sweet and flattering!

COTTIN. Don't I know what I've seen with my own eyes?! Was I mistaken?! Your lover confessed to me. Did he lie? Is everybody a liar?! And now you come along with only your word?! Do you think I'm going to take this lying down? Am I an idiot?

MME. COTTIN. Idiot or not, you're a fool to believe everything that's told you, and then invent the rest yourself!

COTTIN. I imagined the whole thing? I tell you, I saw Monsieur steal out of your room last night? Was I crazy?

MME. COTTIN. Last night?

COTTIN. Yes, Madame, last night! At four in the morning! You know it as well as I!

POUJADE [*to himself*]. Catch them red-handed and they'd cry their innocence to Heaven!

MME. COTTIN [*laughing*]. Last night! I swear by anything you want that not a single person put foot in my room last night!

COTTIN [*with composure*]. Madame, I can't listen to any more of this. I thought that perhaps you were both — forgetful, for a moment — that you — slipped — I should have been glad to have you repent. But I see you're both guiltier than I had thought.

MME. COTTIN. But, Théodore, I swear you're wrong! You must be dreaming! Monsieur was not in my room! [*Turning to Maxime.*] Why don't you defend yourself, Monsieur?

MAXIME [*embarrassed*]. No matter what you may think, Monsieur, I must really —

COTTIN [*to Maxime*]. Shut up! That's all you must really do!

[*Geneviève comes to the drawing-room window, leans out of it, and listens.*]

COTTIN [*to his wife*]. Nathalie! Your defense is useless! You can't have any feelings, for your children or your husband! To receive a lover in your room! A room that even I respect, a room that connects with your daughter's room!

MME. COTTIN. Now, dear, I —

COTTIN. You never thought that your own daughter might —! You're worse than the worst! You ought to be this moment on your knees, and not try to find new lies — everything condemns you.— He was with you yesterday!

[*Geneviève leaves the window, closing it, and disappears quickly.*]

MME. COTTIN [*violently*]. Do you want to know the truth, Théodore, the whole truth? Well, here it is, and God pity you! Monsieur Maxime is my lover, and yesterday is not the first time I've received him. But — we've not seen each other for over a week! So there! Isn't that true, Maxime? [*Maxime acknowledges this by a bow of the head.*] You see?!

COTTIN [*overcome*]. I don't care where or when — I know more now than I wanted to know — keep the other details! It's enough that I'm positive you have a lover. If you want to parade your shame, do it, but not here! My children are not going to have such an example of mother-love near them! Well, [*Authoritatively.*] you're going to leave here at once, both of you; we'll find some excuse to tell the others! Neither of you is going to set foot in this house again. Only honest people have a right here!

MME. COTTIN. Théodore!

MAXIME. Monsieur, listen to me —

COTTIN. Haven't I the right to kill them both, Poujade? I don't want to have any scandal, I tell you. So get out! I'm not going to have you around here! Out with you — into the streets, anywhere — I don't care!

[*Mme. Cottin goes up-stage; Maxime retreats a few steps.*

Geneviève comes in and throws herself at her father's feet.]

GENEVIÈVE. Papa! Forgive her, Papa!

MAXIME. Geneviève!

COTTIN [*to his wife*]. Don't you want the earth to swallow you up, when you see your daughter, your pure and innocent daughter ask forgiveness for you?! Get up, Geneviève darling, your mother is not worth kneeling for. She has soiled our love, yours and mine! But you, you are my consolation — your father needs you now!

POUJADE [*going to Cottin*]. For God's sake, man, brace up! Don't give in now!

GENEVIÈVE. Papa, please, don't accuse Mama — she's not to blame —

MAXIME [*advancing to Cottin*]. Monsieur Cottin, one word —

COTTIN. Silence! My dear child, things are happening now that you can't understand. I must be firm — leave me! Don't make it harder; go back and play your games.

GENEVIÈVE. Papa, Papa! I — I am the only one who is to blame! Forgive *me!*

COTTIN. What's this?

GENEVIÈVE. Maxime — last night — it was my room!

COTTIN [*after a pause*]. Your — room? [*He turns to Maxime, who tries to get away.*] She too!! You, God —[*He siezes Maxime by the throat.*]

POUJADE. Choke him!

GENEVIÈVE [*holding back her father, and clinging to him*]. Papa, don't kill him! He is — think of — my — child —!

[*Geneviève faints. Cottin releases Maxime. Poujade goes to Geneviève, placing her on a chair.*]

POUJADE. The last straw!

COTTIN [*cursing them all*]. Swine! I'm going! Swine!

[*He goes out into the garden and disappears.*]

POUJADE. Help! Help! Hey there! Fournier, help! Water!

MME. COTTIN [*going to Maxime*]. You love her?

MAXIME [*briefly*]. Yes!

MME. COTTIN [*repulsing him*]. Coward!

[*She goes to Geneviève.*

Friends and guests enter precipitately from the house. Dumoulin stops them on the porch.]

POUJADE. Why do you take so long? I've been waiting half an hour for you? Vinegar! Salts! Brandy! The child's fainted!

[*The company disperses; some come downstage by Geneviève.*]

PROSPER [*coming in at the back*]. Mademoiselle Geneviève fainted! [*Furiously, to Maxime.*] Monsieur, you promised to have an explanation with me. I'm waiting for it!

MAXIME. [*trying to rid himself of Prosper*]. Mademoiselle Geneviève will be a mother in six months! Make love to her now!

[CURTAIN.]

ACT III

[*A middle-class dining-room.— Right, a porcelain stove; left, a side-board. A door at the back, and one on each side of the room.— A number of pictures adorn the walls; there are likewise plates hung from the moldings, exposition medals, shields and weapons, framed diplomas, etc.— A table, center, with places for three.*]

FOURNIER [*alone, philosophizing*]. The pâté, omelette, chicken — that will be enough if the ladies don't get back from the country — but if they do —! Oh, what's the odds? They won't be very hungry after that affair yesterday at La Varenne! Think of it —!

[*He shrugs his shoulders and goes about his business.*

Enter Mme. Cottin hurriedly, followed by Geneviève. Both are in traveling attire.]

MME. COTTIN [*excitedly*]. Where is he, Fournier? He isn't dead, is he, Fournier? Tell me!

FOURNIER. No, Madame, Monsieur is here.

MME. COTTIN. Oh, how relieved I am! Geneviève, he's not dead! What's he doing?

FOURNIER. Monsieur has locked himself in his room since this morning.

MME. COTTIN. Who's looking after the shop?

FOURNIER. Monsieur Poujade and his nephew. They're both in a fearful humor; can't say a word to them! Monsieur Poujade insulted me twice this morning, twice! I warn Madame, if this continues I shan't stay!

MME. COTTIN. But have you seen Monsieur this morning?

FOURNIER. No, Madame; when Monsieur Poujade and I arrived by the first train, Monsieur was already in his room.

[*He goes up behind the table.*]

MME. COTTIN [*to Geneviève*]. What can he do now?

GENEVIÈVE [*frightened*]. I don't know: write?

MME. COTTIN. He might kill himself — hang, asphyxiate himself — anything!

FOURNIER [*reassuringly*]. I don't think Monsieur contemplates suicide!

MME. COTTIN. Never mind, Fournier; try to find out what he's doing. Stop him, don't let him do any harm to himself!

FOURNIER. Very well, Madame, I'll keep watch.

[*He goes out.*]

MME. COTTIN [*to Geneviève, who sits down, overcome*]. Poor Papa, poor Théodore! My poor child, what *have* you done! How could you do such a thing, you a child we had so much trouble to educate! We spared nothing for you, at the convent, the expensive boarding-school! You were so modest! Every time you heard a vulgar expression you lowered your eyes! And now we find that Mademoiselle — so that's what your —

GENEVIÈVE [*intrepidly*]. But, Mama, how was I to know —?

MME. COTTIN [*excitedly*]. What you didn't know! Haven't I told you twenty times that you should have no secrets from your mother? That when a young man said things to you you should let me know, and in any case never answer when he made declarations to you! We never tired of dinning it into your ears that all young men try to ruin young girls — that you've got to shun them like the plague! You should never, never believe their oaths and promises. And then if a young lady happens to take a fancy to a young man, is that any reason why —?

GENEVIÈVE. No, Mama, I meant to say — I meant if I'd known you loved him already —

MME. COTTIN. Since when does a mother have to explain her actions to her daughter? And especially in a case like this? For that matter, I'm not — but think of the awful situation for you! How can you hope to marry? Who will take you?

GENEVIÈVE [*rising*]. Maxime! He's promised!

MME. COTTIN. Promised!? [*Aside.*] He's more underhanded than I thought him! The traitor!

GENEVIÈVE [*with growing excitement*]. Anyway, is there anything so out of the way in a young man's loving his fiancée before their marriage? So long as they *do* intend to get married? It was so exciting to have him make love to me in secret — and he was so nice about it! I loved him at once, dreamed about him, thought of nothing in the world but him! One night, perhaps you remember? it was so beautiful, he recited the *Serenade* to us, so sweetly and softly, I was in Heaven! Then he came and whispered in my ear; I couldn't interrupt him; he talked so wonderfully! I was his from that time on; he could ask anything of me! Well, he asked me to come to his rooms the next day for my lesson — and I went!

MME. COTTIN [*sitting down, overcome*]. The monster! I suspected something of the kind, but I never thought he would dishonor you!

GENEVIÈVE. There's nothing dishonorable — Louise Bignolet —

MME. COTTIN. What about Louise Bignolet?

GENEVIÈVE. She had a baby before she was married, and Hortense had a — lover when she was still in boarding-school. Get married afterward, and everything's all right! Of course, there *is* a difference!

MME. COTTIN. What?

GENEVIÈVE [*in an undertone*]. Louise didn't have a mother!

MME. COTTIN [*hiding her face*]. What a curse! It's like Fate!

GENEVIÈVE [*going to her mother, tenderly*]. Mama —

MME. COTTIN [*rises, thrusting Geneviève aside*]. Don't! My dearest child! I hear some one! It's probably your father! Run away, Geneviève, please leave us alone.

GENEVIÈVE. But, Mama —!

MME. COTTIN. Go! [*Geneviève goes out.*] Oh, God, give me the strength to persuade him!

[*Enter Maxime in great haste.*]

MAXIME. What's happened?

MME. COTTIN [*running to him*]. Maxime! He'll kill you!

MAXIME. Let him kill me! I've already given him my life to dispose of!

MME. COTTIN. Maxime, don't provoke him! When a quiet man like Théodore once loses his head you can't tell what he'll do! Listen: so far there's no great harm done. Go away, hide yourself somewhere; don't stay here!

MAXIME. But I've decided to stay! You don't think for a moment I could live away from you two! I'm going to stay!

MME. COTTIN [*supplicatingly*]. If I'm nothing to you any more, then for her sake, for my daughter's sake!

MAXIME [*touched*]. Why speak of Geneviève?

MME. COTTIN. You love her — you love her more than you do me, don't you?

MAXIME [*hesitating*]. Yes, I love her, but it was always you I loved in her; I adored two women in one! Sometimes she was you, sometimes you were she — you were both one! She was to me the perfume of the flower, you were the fruit! What a dream —! Now that it has flown, Nathalie, I have only to — die!

MME. COTTIN. Maxime — I love you!

[*Fournier opens the door half-way.*]

FOURNIER. Madame, Monsieur Maxime, you'd better go into the bed-room or the drawing-room — hide yourselves! Here comes Monsieur!

MAXIME [*firmly*]. Good, we'll have it out now!

MME. COTTIN. Maxime, please come!

MAXIME. I'm going to stay!

MME. COTTIN. For Geneviève's sake — for the sake of the child, come!

[*She tries to drag him out.*]

MAXIME [*resisting*]. No!

COTTIN'S VOICE [*outside*]. Well, Fournier, to-day or to-morrow: when you're ready! I'll wait!

FOURNIER [*to Cottin*]. I'm coming, Monsieur, I'm coming. [*To Mme. Cottin and Maxime.*] You'd better make up your minds — you can come back later if you like. Just treat Monsieur kindly, he's a good-hearted man if you handle him right.

MME. COTTIN. Fournier is right; come, Maxime.

MAXIME [*allowing Mme. Cottin to take him out into the next room*]. Well — if you wish it!

COTTIN'S VOICE [*outside*]. Fournier, *are* you coming to help me?!

[*All go out.*

Enter Cottin in his traveling clothes; he does not wear his decoration.[1] *He has valises and blankets. Fournier likewise is burdened with traveling paraphernalia.*]

COTTIN. Put the valise there — the cash-box over here! Now go and get the hat-box — Wait a moment, go down to the shop and tell Poujade to come up here.

FOURNIER. But, Monsieur, lunch isn't ready yet.

[1] Municipal honorary titles are indicated by decorations worn on the lapel.

COTTIN. It's not for lunch: I want to see him!

[*Fournier goes out.*]

COTTIN [*alone*]. Don't want to forget anything! [*He takes a note-book from his pocket.*] Bills payable for the week: 2500, 120, 1500; there's enough in the cash-box. The Champtonnerre bill will be paid — Nathalie probably sent that! [*Raising his head a moment.*] God! Her deceit! And with a little Latin teacher! And I accused him of working Dodo too hard! And to have the whole lot fool me, while I — damned fool! [*Resuming his calculations.*] All right for bills payable! I'll see about sending a power of attorney for the dissolution of partnership; advise Poujade to take his nephew as partner — Prosper knows a good bit about business! Poor fellow, he loved Nini! There's the man she ought to have married! They'd have carried on the business —"Cottin and Poujade"! — they'd have made a mighty happy couple — and now! [*He rises.*] Work and sweat your life out for your children! — The house in the country, furniture, they can do what they like with them! I don't want to hear about them again! [*Center.*] And to have a thing like this happen to me, the calmest and easiest-going fellow! To me, the head of a family! Me, an honorable business man! There's not a person in Paris can say a word against the firm! And here I am forced to run away like a bankrupt, and hide myself! Oh, Nathalie, how you've abused my confidence, my love!

[*Enter Poujade.*]

POUJADE. What's the matter, old man, are you going away?

COTTIN. Dear old Poujade, yes, I'm going away. I've been thinking the whole matter over — I wandered about last night, trying to decide whether to jump into the Marne or hang myself in the Bois de Vincennes. At sunrise, I found myself in Paris. I was afraid and ashamed of myself. I said it would be foolish to benefit the others in that way, for an honest man to kill himself and let the true culprits live. I don't want to be around the place where I've been dishonored, so I'm going away: abroad, to America. I don't know where! Here's a letter giving you final instructions about my affairs. [*He gives Poujade the letter.*]

POUJADE [*refusing to take it*]. Why, it's impossible!

COTTIN. My dear friend, I simply can't stand all this; another shock like yesterday, and I'd go crazy. I'd much better go away.

POUJADE. It's not so bad as that! Just look at it calmly!

COTTIN. Calmly! Ha! What would you do, *calmly,* if you were in my shoes?!

POUJADE [*hesitating*]. In your shoes? First I'd have killed everybody, and then considered later. But as you didn't have the strength of character to do that, it's — a bit difficult. Let's think it over!

COTTIN. Think as much as you like; the more I think of it, the worse it seems. One of us has to go — I'll sacrifice myself!

POUJADE. You haven't the least idea what you're thinking or talking about. Listen to me: things aren't so bad as you make them out. For the sake of your daughter's reputation you've got to force the man who ruined her to marry her — you have a legal right to kill him! It's very simple: marry them, forgive your daughter, legitimize the child, and then kill the man afterward if you want to!

COTTIN. Kill him! [*Trying to evade the question.*] What if she loves him?

POUJADE. She wouldn't love a man like that!

COTTIN. She's a child, she doesn't know anything about life!

POUJADE. Then it doesn't make a bit of difference one way or the other. Now, about your wife.

COTTIN. Don't talk about her! She's disgraced me! I don't want to see her again!

POUJADE. Kill her!

COTTIN [*outraged*]. Once more, Poujade, we're not butchers here. You keep on telling me to kill her! Arrests! Scandal! Gossip! Trials! Have that happen to a man who's led a decent and honorable life for half a century! No, no, not that! I don't want to hear anything more! You can look after the business! Sell it, make your own terms, I don't care! [*Going to the door and calling.*] Fournier, bring my baggage! [*To Poujade, as he extends his hand to him.*] Good-by, old man!

POUJADE [*turning his back to Cottin*]. I see through your trick — you don't want to hear — no!! You're leaving me your wife and daughter, your business, and then tell me, "Fix it up as well as you can!" What if I went away, too?

COTTIN. Can't you understand, the very sight of this place is poison to me!? Hurry, Nathalie may come in any moment! Now read that. [*He hands him the letter.*] I'm going! [*He goes toward the door.*] Fournier! Fournier!

[*In coming back, he catches sight of his wife, who has just entered.*]

MME. COTTIN [*holding a handkerchief to her eyes*]. Théodore!

COTTIN [*in despair*]. You see, Poujade? What did I tell you?

MME. COTTIN [*tearfully*]. Théodore, if a guilty woman has any right to be heard, listen to me — please!!

[*Cottin turns around and makes as if to go out.*]

POUJADE. Listen to what she has to say, Cottin!

COTTIN [*firmly*]. Never!

MME. COTTIN [*falling to her knees*]. Théodore!

COTTIN [*with dignity*]. Don't imagine, Madame, I am one of those men you can soften by tears! Don't deceive yourself by thinking I'll believe your story! How do I know you haven't always been faithless to me — since we were married? How do I know you're not acting a part this minute? No, I won't listen!

MME. COTTIN. Théodore, don't go away! Do anything you want to me; I'll bear it. I know I don't deserve to be forgiven, you ought to punish me — if you do, I'll not complain. I'm asking you, imploring you, for Geneviève's sake, not mine!

COTTIN [*brutally*]. I forbid you to mention her name in my presence! Your own daughter that you gave to your lover!

MME. COTTIN. Oh!

COTTIN. I took you to be my faithful partner; you deceived me. Therefore I have nothing more to do with you! Go back to the miserable life you lived before I married you! But Geneviève is my daughter, my own flesh and blood, she's dearest to me of anything on earth — and you've ruined her! Don't drag her in! I won't let you!

MME. COTTIN. I'm not trying to drag her in! It's just for her happiness!

[*Enter Fournier.*]

FOURNIER. Monsieur called me?

COTTIN. Yes; take my bags down-stairs.

POUJADE. Cottin, think it over! Don't do anything rash!

COTTIN [*to Poujade*]. I'm going to be firm! [*To Fournier.*] Do what I tell you! [*To Mme. Cottin.*] You — say what you have to say, at once! I'm in a hurry!

[*Fournier goes out.*]

MME. COTTIN [*rising*]. Why are you leaving?

COTTIN. That's my affair! I know what I'm going to do.

MME. COTTIN. Then you're leaving us all! If you leave your daughter, what'll become of her? Without any one to look after her — and her child?

COTTIN. She will have you! You've guided her beautifully so far —! It will serve you right!

MME. COTTIN [*after a pause*]. Geneviève is your child, your own flesh and blood! Do you want her to be the laughing-stock of the whole neighborhood? And you! your daughter, with her bastard, do you want her to be driven to the streets?

COTTIN [*defending himself*]. Of course — I don't want her to be —

POUJADE. Well, if you leave —

COTTIN [*after a pause*]. If I leave, that's no reason why —

MME. COTTIN. You don't want it to be said, Théodore, that you, the honorable Monsieur Cottin, drove his daughter into a shameful life — just because of his pride!

POUJADE [*to Cottin*]. Pure selfishness, I call it!

COTTIN [*after a pause*]. You think so?

POUJADE. Yes. Don't you see, Geneviève will still bear your name?

MME. COTTIN. You're shirking your duties as a father!

COTTIN [*sitting down, his hands pressed to his forehead*]. Tell me, then, advise me, what shall I do?

MME. COTTIN. Marry them.

POUJADE. Think it over afterward.

COTTIN. Marry them? But what do we know of this Champanet? He's a teacher, but who is he? Where does he come from? He hasn't a sou to his name!

POUJADE. You haven't got many husbands to choose from!

MME. COTTIN. Monsieur Champanet comes from a very good family; some day he'll have a noble name, and when his uncle dies he comes in for a very respectable fortune.

COTTIN [*nearly convinced*]. Yes, yes, that's all right. But this man is your lover!

MME. COTTIN. So you want to make a scandal? Everybody knows now that Monsieur Champanet is Geneviève's lover. That wouldn't lead them to suspect anything else. If you want a scandal, very well, make one! Never mind about your daughter and family!

COTTIN [*hesitating*]. How about it, Poujade, d'you think I ought to marry them off?

POUJADE. I've told you — Kill 'em afterward if you like.

MME. COTTIN [*to Poujade, terrified*]. Kill Maxime?!

POUJADE. Certainly. Hasn't a husband the legal right to do that?

MME. COTTIN. But after the marriage?

POUJADE [*aside to Mme. Cottin*]. Between you and me, marriage makes very little difference!

MME. COTTIN [*outraged*]. Don't listen to him, Théodore, marry them; and then if any one has to make a sacrifice, let me! I'm to blame, her mother: I'll go away — go into a nunnery — and die there! [*She cries.*]

COTTIN [*after a moment's reflection*]. Poujade, what do you think?

POUJADE. That's one way.

COTTIN [*deciding, with determination*]. Well, if everybody wants it, marry them!

MME. COTTIN [*throwing herself into Cottin's arms*]. Oh, thank you! thank you! You're a saint! [*She kisses his hands. Cottin rises, opens the bedroom door, and his wife speaks to Geneviève and Maxime.*] Come here, children, thank your father — he's forgiven you — you can marry now!

[*Enter Geneviève precipitately; she throws herself into her father's arms. Maxime follows her and stops at some distance.*]

GENEVIÈVE. Oh, Papa, how good you are — and how happy I am!

COTTIN [*seriously*]. Monsieur, since you have already *taken* my daughter, I give her to you as your wife. She is yours! Take her away!

MAXIME [*hesitating*]. I cannot accept!

COTTIN [*amazed*]. Why, please?

MAXIME. I — I am not worthy of her.

COTTIN. You —?

MAXIME. I see very plainly that you despise me: you tell me to "take her away"! When I'm her husband you will refuse to see her, you will despise her because she is my wife. For the sake of your family honor, give her a husband she won't have to be ashamed of!

COTTIN. But — the child?

MAXIME. This is a matter which concerns her whole life.

COTTIN [*solemnly*]. Luckily for us, we don't hold the same opinions as you. We have our prejudices, and our old-fashioned ideas, and one of them is that we insist on having our children recognized by the father. You're going to marry my daughter to make this possible — as Poujade says — I insist, I command! If my daughter is not happy, so much the worse for her; it's all her own doing. I must confess that as a son-in-law, I might do worse. And perhaps some day you'll live down what you've done, but —

GENEVIÈVE. Papa, we love you so much! We'll do anything —

COTTIN [*in an undertone*]. And what you've done, Monsieur, is — is little better than — incest!

MAXIME. You see, then, Monsieur, this marriage is impossible.

COTTIN [*in great perplexity*]. Yes — but yet —

[*Enter Fournier.*]

COTTIN [*suddenly to Fournier*]. What do you want, Fournier?

FOURNIER. To serve lunch; it's twelve o'clock.

COTTIN. Leave us.— Wait a moment, bring up my bags, I'm not going away.

FOURNIER [*smiling*]. I never took them down. [*He goes out.*]

COTTIN [*considering*]. Have them all here — in the same house? With my daughter in her position! Impossible! Everybody would talk about it! What wouldn't Dumoulin say, and the Boulards!

MAXIME. We are going to do our best to live down the past, Monsieur Cottin — there's no need to send any one away.

COTTIN [*to Poujade*]. What do you think?

POUJADE. Do whatever you like; I've told you what I think; I wash my hands of the whole affair.

COTTIN. Geneviève is not so much to blame — I forgive her — she didn't know. [*Indicating Maxime.*] Perhaps I can forgive you some day. And to think of the havoc you made in my home, with my —! [*Looking at his wife.*] Nathalie, you are bound to me by oaths — Maxime swore nothing! — my honor, the honor of the family — they were in your keeping. A man can't forget those things soon!

POUJADE [*shrugging his shoulders*]. Why not *her* too, while you're at it!!

COTTIN. You really —?

GENEVIÈVE [*kissing her father*]. Dear, dear Papa!

COTTIN [*moved*]. They're all against me! [*He puts his hand over his eyes and sobs.*] Nathalie!

MME. COTTIN [*kissing his hand*]. You're good! You're generous!

POUJADE [*cynically*]. I thought so!

COTTIN [*to Maxime, who takes Geneviève by the hand*]. You have a great deal to answer for!

[*Enter Prosper hastily.*]

PROSPER. Monsieur, the Count de Melimbec has come again for his chronometer. He insists on seeing you!

COTTIN [*with resignation*]. Tell him to go to the devil! To-day I'm going to be with my family — my daughter is going to be married. [*With a sigh.*]

PROSPER [*with amazement*]. Mademoiselle Geneviève —!

COTTIN [*to Prosper*]. That's so, poor Prosper! We forgot about you altogether. [*He holds out his hand to him.*]

MME. COTTIN. Dear Prosper!

GENEVIÈVE. Poor Monsieur Prosper!

POUJADE [*who has gone to his nephew; aside to him*]. Happy Prosper!

COTTIN [*a little cheered up*]. Well, he'll be of the family anyway, we'll give him cousin Boulard, won't we? Cousin Boulard! Nice little Célina! I think you'll hit it off nicely, you two!

POUJADE [*aside*]. Yes, that's a wonderful plan, you old —!

COTTIN [*to Poujade, slapping him on the shoulder*]. You mountain bear, see, you don't have to cut throats to have things turn out beautifully! Nobody's dead. [*Gravely.*] Only I make one condition to this marriage [*All surround Cottin*] and that is that nothing's to be said about it. We needn't have the neighborhood gossiping! Ah! [*He puts his decoration back in his button-hole.*] Now, let's have lunch, children! Fournier, three more places and some of our best wine: we don't marry our daughters off every day —! [*Fournier sets the extra places, and the company sits at the table.*]

MME. COTTIN [*simply, to Maxime*]. Sit by me — son-in-law!

[CURTAIN.]

Françoise' Luck

(*La Chance de Françoise*)

A Comedy in One Act

By

GEORGES DE PORTO-RICHE

TRANSLATED BY

BARRETT H. CLARK

Presented for the first time, in Paris, at the Théâtre Libre, December 10, 1888.

PERSONS REPRESENTED:

	CAST AT *Théâtre Libre*
MARCEL DESROCHES	Henri Mayer
GUÉRIN	Laury
JEAN	Antoine
FRANÇOISE	Mmes. Sigall
MADELEINE	Lucy Manvel

	CAST AT *Gymnase*
MARCEL DESROCHES	Pierre Achard
GUÉRIN	M. Bréant
JEAN	L. Debray
FRANÇOISE	Mmes. Julia Depoix
MADELEINE	Silviac

	CAST AT *Comédie-Française*
MARCEL DESROCHES	Le Bargy
GUÉRIN	Laroche
JEAN	Falconnier
FRANÇOISE	Mmes. Bertiny
MADELEINE	Ludwig

The scene is Auteuil. The time is the present.

FRANÇOISE' LUCK

[*A studio. At the back is a door opening upon a garden; doors to the right and left; also a small inconspicuous door to the left. There are a few pictures on easels. The table is littered with papers, books, weapons, bric-a-brac, here and there; chairs and sofas. It is eleven o'clock in the morning.*]

FRANÇOISE [*a small woman, frail, with a melancholy look, at times rather mocking. As the curtain rises she is alone. She raises and lowers the window-blind from time to time*]. A little more! There! Oh, the sunlight! How blinding! [*Glancing at the studio with an air of satisfaction.*] How neat everything is! [*In attempting to take something from the table, she knocks some papers to the floor.*] Well! [*Seeing a letter, among the papers which she is picking up.*] A letter! From M. Guérin — [*Reading.*] "My dear friend, why do you persist in keeping silence? You say very little of the imprudent woman who has dared to become the companion of the handsome Marcel! Do you recompense her for her confidence in you, for her courage? You are not at all like other men: your frivolity, if you will permit the term, your —" [*Interrupting herself.*] He writes the word! [*Continuing.*] "Your cynicism makes me tremble for you. Absent for a year! How much friendship is gone to waste! Why were we thrust apart the moment you were married? Why did my wife's health make sunlight an absolute necessity for her? We are now leaving Rome; in a month I'll drop in on you at Auteuil —" [*Interrupting herself again.*] Very soon!

[*Marcel appears at the back.*]

" I am very impatient to see you, and very anxious to see Madame Desroches. I wonder whether she will take to me? I hope she will. Take care, you ruffian, I shall cross-question her carefully, and if I find the slightest cloud in her happiness, her friend-to-be will be an angry man." [*She stops reading, and says to herself, sadly.*] A friend — I should like that!

MARCEL [*carelessly dressed. He is of the type which usually appeals to women*]. Ah, inquisitive, you read my letters?

FRANÇOISE. Oh, it's an old one —

MARCEL [*chaffing her*]. From Guérin?

FRANÇOISE. I found it there, when I was putting the studio in order.

MARCEL [*tenderly*]. The little romantic child is looking for a friend?

FRANÇOISE. I have so much to tell, so much about my recent happiness!

MARCEL. Am I not that friend?

FRANÇOISE. You are the man I love. Should I consult with you, when your happiness is at stake?

MARCEL. Too deep for me! [*Yawning.*] Oh, I'm tired —!

FRANÇOISE. Did you come in late last night?

MARCEL. Three o'clock.

FRANÇOISE. You were quiet about it, you naughty man!

MARCEL. Were you jealous?

FRANÇOISE. The idea! I am morally certain that you love no one except your wife.

MARCEL [*sadly*]. It's true, I love no one except my wife —

FRANÇOISE [*chaffing him in turn*]. Poor Marcel!

MARCEL. I was bored to death at that supper; I can't imagine why.— They all tell me I'm getting stout.

FRANÇOISE. That's no reason why you shouldn't please.

MARCEL. God is very unjust.

FRANÇOISE. So they say!

MARCEL [*stretching out on a sofa*]. Excuse my appearance, won't you, Françoise? [*Making himself comfortable.*] I can't keep my eyes open any longer nowadays — The days of my youth — Why, I was — [*He stops.*]

FRANÇOISE. You were just the right age for marriage.

MARCEL [*as if to banish the idea*]. Oh! [*A pause.*] I'm sure you will get along well with Guérin. Yours are kindred spirits — you're alike — not in looks, however.

FRANÇOISE. Morally, you mean?

MARCEL. Yes — I'm flattering him by the comparison.

FRANÇOISE. He's like this, then: sentimental, a good friend, and an honest man. Yes, I think I shall get along nicely with him.

MARCEL. What a sympathetic nature you have! You've never seen him, and you know him already.

FRANÇOISE. How long has he been married?

MARCEL. He was born married!

FRANÇOISE. Tell me.

MARCEL. Ten years, I think.

FRANÇOISE. He's happy?

MARCEL. Very.

FRANÇOISE. What sort of woman is she?

MARCEL. Lively.

FRANÇOISE. Though virtuous?

MARCEL. So they say.

FRANÇOISE. Then Madame Guérin and the handsome Martel — eh?

MARCEL. A friend's wife?

FRANÇOISE. It's very tempting — [*Marcel seems to take this in bad spirit; he is about to put on his hat.*] Are you going out?

MARCEL. I lunch at the club.

FRANÇOISE. Very well.

MARCEL. I'm all — a little nervous; I need a breath of air.

FRANÇOISE. Paris air!

MARCEL. Precisely.

FRANÇOISE. And your work —?

MARCEL. I'm not in the mood.

FRANÇOISE. There's only ten days before the Salon: you'll never be ready.

MARCEL. What chance have I, with my talent?

FRANÇOISE. You have a great deal of talent — it's recognized everywhere.

MARCEL. I did have —

[*A pause.*]

FRANÇOISE. Will you be home for dinner?

MARCEL [*tenderly*]. Of course! And don't let any black suspicions get the better of you: I'm not lunching with anybody!

FRANÇOISE. I suspect you?!

MARCEL [*gratefully*]. 'Til later, then! [*A pause. Frankly.*] Of course, I don't always go where I tell you I'm going. Why should I worry you? But if you think I — do what I ought not to do, you are mistaken. I'm no longer a bachelor, you know.

FRANÇOISE. Just a trifle, aren't you?

MARCEL. No jealousy, dear! The day of adventures is dead and buried. Thirty-five mortal years, scarcity of hair, a noticeable rotundity, and married! Opportunities are fewer now!

FRANÇOISE [*playfully*]. Don't lose courage, your luck may return — A minute would suffice.

MARCEL [*mournfully*]. I don't dare hope.

FRANÇOISE. Married! You were never fated to be a proprietor, you are doomed to be a tenant.

MARCEL [*as he is about to leave, he sees a telegram on the table*]. Oh, a telegram, and you said nothing to me about it!

FRANÇOISE. I didn't see it. Jean must have brought it while you were asleep.

MARCEL. From Passy! I know that hand! [*Aside, with surprise.*] Madame Guérin — Madeleine! Well! [*Reading.*] "My dear friend, I lunch to-day with my aunt Madame de Monglat, at La Muette — as I used to. Come and see me before noon, I have serious things to talk over with you." [*He stops reading; aside, much pleased.*] A rendezvous! And after three years! Poor Guérin! — No! It wouldn't be decent, now! No!

FRANÇOISE [*aside*]. He seems to be waking up!

MARCEL [*aside*]. They must have returned! Françoise was right — a minute would suffice! The dear girl!

FRANÇOISE. No bad news?

MARCEL [*in spite of himself*]. On the contrary!

FRANÇOISE. Oh!

MARCEL [*embarrassed*]. It's from that American woman who saw my picture the other day — at Goupil's, you remember? She insists that I give it to her for ten thousand francs. I really think I'll let her have it. Nowadays you never can tell —

FRANÇOISE. I think you would be very wise to sell.

MARCEL [*handing her the telegram*]. Don't you believe me?

FRANÇOISE. Absolutely.

[*Marcel puts the telegram in his pocket. A pause.*]

MARCEL [*hesitating before he leaves; aside*]. She's a darling; a perfect little darling.

FRANÇOISE. Then you're not going out?

MARCEL [*surprised*]. Do you want to send me away?

FRANÇOISE. If you're going out to lunch, you had better hurry — the train leaves in a few minutes.

MARCEL [*becoming suddenly affectionate*]. How can I hurry when you are so charming? You're adorable this morning!

FRANÇOISE. D'you think so?

[*A pause.*]

MARCEL [*aside*]. Curious, but every time I have a rendezvous, she's that way!

FRANÇOISE. Good-by, then; I've had enough of you! If you stay you'll upset all my plans. I'd quite made up my mind to be melancholy and alone. It's impossible to be either gay or sad with you! Run along!

MARCEL [*taking off his hat, which he had put on some moments before*]. I tell you this is my house, and this my studio. Your house is there by the garden.

FRANÇOISE. Yes, it's only there that you are my husband.

MARCEL [*contradicting her*]. Oh! [*Reproachfully, and with tenderness.*] Tell me, Françoise, why don't you ever want to go out with me?

FRANÇOISE. You know I don't like society.

MARCEL. I'm seen so much alone!

FRANÇOISE. So much the better for you; you will be taken for a bachelor!

MARCEL. One might think to hear you that husband and wife ought never to live together.

FRANÇOISE. Perhaps I should see you oftener if we weren't married!

MARCEL. Isn't it a pleasure to you, Madame, to be in the arms of your husband?

FRANÇOISE. Isn't it likewise a pleasure to be able to say, " He is free, I am not his wife, he is not my husband; I am not his duty, a millstone around his neck; I am his avocation, his love? If he leaves me, I know he is tired of me, but if he comes back, then I know he loves me."

MARCEL. Françoise, you are an extremist!

FRANÇOISE. You think so?

MARCEL. You are!

FRANÇOISE. And then —?

MARCEL. I know your philosophy is nothing but love. [*A pause.*] You cry sometimes, don't you? When I'm not here?

FRANÇOISE. Just a little.

MARCEL. I must make you very unhappy! When you are sad, don't hide it from me, Françoise; one of your tears would force me to do anything in the world for you.

FRANÇOISE. One, yes! But, many —?

MARCEL. Don't make fun of me: I am serious. If I told you that my affection for you is as great as yours, I —

FRANÇOISE. You would be lying.

MARCEL. That may be! But it seems to me I adore you! Every time I leave you, I feel so lonely; I wander about like a lost soul! I think that something must be happening to you. And when I come home at midnight, and open the door, I feel an exquisite sensation — Is that love? You ought to know — you are so adept!

FRANÇOISE. Perhaps.

MARCEL [*unthinkingly*]. You know, Françoise, one can never be sure of one's self.

FRANÇOISE. Of course!

MARCEL. No one can say, " I love to-day, and

I shall love to-morrow." You no more than any one else.

FRANÇOISE [*offended*]. I?

MARCEL. How can you tell, whether in fifteen years —?

FRANÇOISE. Oh, I'm a little child — I'm different from the others — I shall always love the same man all his life. But go on, you were saying —?

MARCEL. Nothing. I want you to be happy, in spite of everything — no matter what may happen — no matter what I may do.

FRANÇOISE. Even if you should deceive me?

MARCEL [*tenderly*]. Deceive you? Never! I care nothing about other women! You are happiness — not a mere pastime.

FRANÇOISE. Alas!

MARCEL. Why alas?

FRANÇOISE. Because it is easier to do without happiness than pleasure.

MARCEL [*tenderly*]. Oh, you are all that is highest and best in my life — I prefer you to everything else! Let a woman come between us, and she will have me to deal with! Call it selfishness, if you will, or egotism — but your peace of mind is an absolute necessity to me!

FRANÇOISE. You need not prepare me for the future, you bad boy; I resigned myself to "possibilities" some time ago. I'm inexperienced and young in years, but I'm older than you.

MARCEL. Shall I tell you something? I never deserved you!

FRANÇOISE. That's true.

MARCEL. When I think how happy you might have made some good and worthy man, and that —

FRANÇOISE. Who then would have made me happy?

MARCEL. You are not happy now.

FRANÇOISE. I didn't marry for happiness; I married in order to have you.

MARCEL. I'm a fool! — It would be nice, wouldn't it, if I were an unfaithful husband!

FRANÇOISE. I'm sure you will never be that.

MARCEL. Do you really think so?

FRANÇOISE. I am positive. What would be the use in deceiving me? I should be so unhappy, and you wouldn't be a bit happier.

MARCEL. You are right.

FRANÇOISE. No, you will not deceive me. To begin with, I have a great deal of luck.

MARCEL [*gaily*]. Of course you have; you don't know how much!

FRANÇOISE [*coquettishly*]. Tell me!

MARCEL. What a child you are!

FRANÇOISE. I've run risks, haven't I?

MARCEL. I should think so! Sometimes I imagine that my happiness does not lie altogether in those sparkling eyes of yours, and I try to fall in love with another woman; I get deeper and deeper for a week or two, and think I am terribly infatuated. But just as I am about to take the fatal leap, I fail: Françoise' luck, you see! At bottom, I'm a commencer; I can't imagine what it is that saves me — and you. Sometimes *she* has done something to displease me, sometimes a divine word from your lips — and a mere nothing, something quite insignificant! For instance, Wednesday, I missed the train, and I came back and had dinner with you. You see, Françoise' luck!

FRANÇOISE. Then you're not going out to-day, are you?

MARCEL. Nor to-morrow; the whole day is yours. We'll close the door!

FRANÇOISE. Aren't you happy?

MARCEL [*kissing her behind the ear*]. Hurry up, you lazy child!

FRANÇOISE. I'm not pretty, but I have my good points.

MARCEL. Not pretty?

FRANÇOISE. No, but I deserve to be.

[*Madeleine appears at the back.*]

MADELEINE. I beg your pardon!

[*Françoise gives an exclamation of surprise and escapes through the door to the right without looking a second time at the visitor.*]

MARCEL [*surprised*]. Madeleine!

[*A pause.*]

MADELEINE [*stylishly dressed. With an air of bravura*]. So this is the way you deceive me!

MARCEL [*gaily*]. My dear, if you think that during these three years —

MADELEINE. I beg your pardon for interrupting your little *tête-à-tête,* Marcel, but your door was open, and I found no servant to announce me.

MARCEL. You know you are always welcome here.

MADELEINE. Your wife is very attractive.

MARCEL. Isn't she? Shall I introduce you?

MADELEINE. Later — I've come to see *you.*

MARCEL. I must confess your visit is a little surprising.

MADELEINE. Especially after my sending that telegram this morning. I thought I should prefer not to trouble you.

MARCEL [*uncertain*]. Ah!

MADELEINE. Yes.

MARCEL. Well?

MADELEINE. Well, no!

MARCEL. I'm sorry. [*Kissing her hand.*] I'm glad to see you, at any rate.

MADELEINE. Same studio as always, eh?

MARCEL. You are still as charming as ever.

MADELEINE. You are as handsome as ever.

MARCEL. I can say no less for you.

MADELEINE. I'm only twenty-eight.

MARCEL. But your husband is fifty: that keeps you young. How long have you been back?

MADELEINE. A week.

MARCEL. And I haven't seen Guérin yet!

MADELEINE. There's no hurry.

MARCEL. What's the matter?

MADELEINE. He's a bit troubled: you know how jealous he is! Well, yesterday, when I was out, he went through all my private papers —

MARCEL. Naturally he came across some letters.

MADELEINE. *The* letters, my dear!

MARCEL. Mine?

MADELEINE. Yes.— [*Gesture from Marcel.*] Old letters.

MARCEL. You kept them?

MADELEINE. From a celebrity? Of course!
MARCEL. The devil!
MADELEINE. Ungrateful!
MARCEL. I beg your pardon —
MADELEINE. You can imagine my explanation following the discovery. My dear Marcel, there's going to be a divorce.
MARCEL. A —! A divorce?
MADELEINE. Don't pity me too much. After all, I shall be free — almost happy.
MARCEL. What resignation!
MADELEINE. Only —
MARCEL. Only what?
MADELEINE. He is going to send you his seconds.
MARCEL [*gaily*]. A duel? — To-day? You're not serious?
MADELEINE. I think he wants to kill you.
MARCEL. But that was an affair of three years ago! Why, to begin with, he hasn't the right!
MADELEINE. Because of the lapse of time?
MARCEL. Three years is three years.
MADELEINE. You're right: *now* you are not in love with his wife: you love your own. Time has changed everything. Now your own happiness is all-sufficient. I can easily understand your indignation against my husband.
MARCEL. Oh, I —
MADELEINE. My husband is slow but he's sure, isn't he?
MARCEL. You're cruel, Madeleine.
MADELEINE. If it's ancient history for you, it's only too recent for him!
MARCEL. Let's not speak about him!

MADELEINE. But he should be a very interesting topic of conversation just now!

MARCEL. I hadn't foreseen his being so cut up.

MADELEINE. You must tell him how sorry you are when you see him.

MARCEL. At the duel?

MADELEINE. Elsewhere!

MARCEL. Where? Here, in my house?

MADELEINE. My dear, he may want to tell you what he feels.

[*A pause.*]

MARCEL [*aside, troubled*]. The devil!—And Françoise? [*Another pause.*] Oh, a duel! Well, I ought to risk my life for you; you have done the same thing for me many times.

MADELEINE. Oh, I was not so careful as you were then.

MARCEL. You are not telling me everything, Madeleine. What put it into your husband's head to look through your papers?

MADELEINE. Ah!

MARCEL. Well, evidently *I* couldn't have excited his jealousy. For a long time he has had no reason to suspect me! Were they my letters he was looking for?

MADELEINE. That is my affair!

MARCEL. Then I am expiating for some one else?

MADELEINE. I'm afraid so.

MARCEL. Perfect!

MADELEINE. Forgive me!

MARCEL [*reproachfully*]. So you are deceiving him!?

MADELEINE. You are a perfect friend today!

MARCEL. Then you really have a lover?

MADELEINE. A second lover! That would be disgraceful, wouldn't it?

MARCEL. The first step is the one with the worst consequences.

MADELEINE. What are you smiling at?

MARCEL. Oh, the happiness of others —! Well, let's have no bitterness.

MADELEINE. No, you might feel remorse!

MARCEL. Oh, Madeleine, why am I not the guilty one this time — you are always so beautiful!

MADELEINE. Your fault! You should have kept what you had!

MARCEL. I thought you were tired of me.

MADELEINE. You will never know what I suffered; I cried like an abandoned shopgirl!

MARCEL. Not for long, though?

MADELEINE. Three months. When I think I once loved you so much, and here I am before you so calm and indifferent! You look like anybody else now. How funny, how disgusting life is! You meet some one, do no end of foolish and wicked and mean things in order to belong to him, and the day comes when you don't know one another. Each takes his turn! I think it would have been better — [*Gesture from Marcel.*] Yes — I ought to try to forget everything.

MARCEL. That's all buried in the past! Wasn't it worth the trouble, the suffering that we have to undergo now?

MADELEINE. You too! You have to recall —!

MARCEL. I'm sorry, but I didn't begin this conversation —

MADELEINE. Never mind! It's all over, let's say nothing more about it!

MARCEL. No, please! Let's — curse me, Madeleine, say anything you like about me — I deserve it all!

MADELEINE. Stop! Behave yourself, you married man! What if your wife heard you!

MARCEL. She? Dear child! She is much too afraid of what I might say to listen.

MADELEINE. Dear child! You cynic! I'll wager you have not been a model husband since your marriage!

MARCEL. You are mistaken there, my dear.

MADELEINE. You are lying!

MARCEL. Seriously; and I'm more surprised than you at the fact — but it's true.

MADELEINE. Poor Marcel!

MARCEL. I do suffer!

MADELEINE. Then you are a faithful husband?

MARCEL. I am frivolous and — compromising — that is all.

MADELEINE. It's rather funny: you seem somehow to be ready to belong to some one!

MARCEL. Madeleine, you are the first who has come near tempting me.

MADELEINE. Is it possible?

MARCEL. I feel myself weakening.

MADELEINE. Thank you so much for thinking of me, dear,— I appreciate it highly, but for the time being, I'll — consider.

MARCEL. Have you made up your mind?

MADELEINE. We shall see later; I'll think it over — perhaps! Yet, I rather doubt if —! You haven't been nice to me to-day, your open honest face hasn't pleased me at all. Then you're so carelessly dressed! I don't think you're at all interesting any more. No, I hardly think so!

MARCEL. But, Madeleine —

MADELEINE. Don't call me Madeleine.

MARCEL. Madame Guérin! Madame Guérin! if I told you how much your telegram meant to me! How excited I was! I trembled when I read it!

MADELEINE. I'll warrant you read it before your wife?

MARCEL. It was so charming of you!

MADELEINE. How depraved you are!

MARCEL. How well you know me!

MADELEINE. Fool!

MARCEL. I adore you!

MADELEINE. That's merely a notion of yours! You imagine that since you haven't seen me for so long — I've just come back from a long trip!

MARCEL. Don't shake my faith in you!

MADELEINE. Think of your duties, my dear; don't forget —

MARCEL. Of my children? I have none.

MADELEINE. Of your wife.

MARCEL [*in desperation*]. You always speak of her!

MADELEINE. Love her, my friend, and if my husband doesn't kill you to-morrow, continue to love her in peace and quiet. You are made for a virtuous life now — any one can see that. I'm flattering you when I consider you a libertine. You've been spoiled by too much happiness, that's the trouble with you!

MARCEL [*trying to kiss her*]. Madeleine, if you only —!

MADELEINE [*evading him*]. Are you out of your wits?

MARCEL. Forgive me: I haven't quite forgotten —! Well, if I am killed it will be for a good reason.

MADELEINE. Poor dear!

MARCEL. It will! This duel is going to compromise you fearfully. Come now, every one will accuse you to-morrow; what difference does it make to you?

MADELEINE. I'm not in the mood!

MARCEL. Now *you* are lying!

MADELEINE. I don't love you.

MARCEL. Nonsense! You're sulking!

MADELEINE. How childish! Don't touch me!! You want me to be unfaithful to everybody! Never! [*Changing.*] Yet —! No; it would be too foolish! Good-by!

MARCEL [*kissing her as she tries to pass him*]. Not before —

MADELEINE. Oh, you've mussed my hat; how awkward of you! [*Trying to escape from Marcel's embrace.*] Let me go!

MARCEL [*jokingly*]. Let you go? In a few days!

MADELEINE. Good-by! My husband may come any moment —

MARCEL. Are you afraid?

MADELEINE. Yes, I'm afraid he might forgive me!

MARCEL. One minute more!

MADELEINE. No! I have just time — I'm going away this evening —

MARCEL. Going away?

MADELEINE. To London.

MARCEL. With — *him,* the other?

MADELEINE. I hope so.

MARCEL. Who knows? He may be waiting this moment for you at Madame de Montglat's, your aunt's —

MADELEINE. They are playing cards together —

MARCEL. The way we are! What a family!

MADELEINE. Impudent!

MARCEL. That's why you came.

MADELEINE [*about to leave*]. Shall I go out through the models' door, as I used to?

MARCEL. If I were still a bachelor you wouldn't leave me like this! You would miss your train this evening — I'll tell you that!

MADELEINE. You may very well look at that long sofa! No, no, my dear: not to-day, thanks!

MARCEL. In an hour, then, at Madame de Montglat's!

MADELEINE. Take care, or I'll make you meet your successor!

MARCEL. Then I can see whether you are still a woman of taste!

MADELEINE. Ah, men are very — I'll say the word after I leave. [*She goes out through the little door.*]

MARCEL [*alone*]. "Men are very —!" If we were, the women would have a very stupid time of it!

[*He is about to follow Madeleine.*]

[*Enter Françoise.*]

FRANÇOISE. Who was that stylish looking woman who just left, Marcel?

MARCEL [*embarrassed*]. Madame Jackson, my American friend.

FRANÇOISE. Well?

MARCEL. My picture? Sold!

FRANÇOISE. Ten thousand? Splendid! Don't you think so? You don't seem very happy!

MARCEL. The idea!

[*He picks up his hat.*]

FRANÇOISE [*jealously*]. Are you going to leave me?

MARCEL. I am just going to Goupil's and tell him.

FRANÇOISE. Then I'll have to lunch all by myself? [*Marcel stops an instant before the mirror.*] You look lovely.

MARCEL [*turning round*]. I —

FRANÇOISE. Oh, you'll succeed —!

[*A pause.*]

MARCEL [*enchanted, in spite of himself*]. What can you be thinking of! [*Aside.*] What if she were after all my happiness?! [*Reproachfully.*] Now Françoise —

FRANÇOISE. I was only joking.

MARCEL [*ready to leave*]. No moping, remember? I can't have that!

FRANÇOISE. I know!

MARCEL [*tenderly. He stands at the threshold. Aside*]. Poor child! — Well! I *may* fail!

[*He goes out, left.*]

FRANÇOISE [*sadly*]. Where is he going? Probably to a rendezvous. Oh, if he is! Will my luck fail me to-day? Soon he'll come back again, well satisfied with himself! I talk to him so much about my resignation, I wonder whether he believes in it? Why must I be tormented this way forever?

[*Enter Jean, with a visiting-card in his hand.*]

JEAN. Is Monsieur not here?

FRANÇOISE. Let me see!

[*She takes the card.*]

JEAN. The gentleman is waiting, Madame.

FRANÇOISE. Ask him to come in. Quick, now!

[*Jean goes out.*]

[*Enter Guérin, at the back. As he sees Françoise he hesitates before coming to her.*]

FRANÇOISE [*cordially*]. Come in, Monsieur. I have never seen you, but I know you very well, already.

GUÉRIN [*a large, strong man, with grayish hair*]. Thank you, Madame. I thought I should find M. Desroches at home. If you will excuse me —

FRANÇOISE. I beg you —!

GUÉRIN. I fear I am intruding: it's so early.

FRANÇOISE. You intruding in Marcel's home?!

GUÉRIN. Madame —

FRANÇOISE. My husband will return soon, Monsieur.

GUÉRIN [*brightening*]. Ah, good!

FRANÇOISE. Will you wait for him here in the studio?

GUÉRIN [*advancing*]. Really, Madame, I should be very ungrateful were I to refuse your kindness.

FRANÇOISE. Here are magazines and newspapers — I shall ask to be excused. [*As she is about to leave.*] It was rather difficult to make you stay!

GUÉRIN. Forgive me, Madame. [*Aside ironically.*] Too bad —! She's decidedly charming!

[*Having gone up-stage, Françoise suddenly retraces her steps.*]

FRANÇOISE. It seems a little strange to you, Monsieur — doesn't it? — to see a woman in this bachelor studio — quite at home?

GUÉRIN. Why, Madame —

FRANÇOISE. Before leaving you alone — which I shall do in a moment — you must know that there is one woman who is very glad to know you have returned to Paris!

GUÉRIN. We just arrived this week.

FRANÇOISE. Good!

GUÉRIN [*ironically*]. It's so long since I've seen Marcel —

FRANÇOISE. Three years.

GUÉRIN. So many things have happened since!

FRANÇOISE. You find him a married man, for one thing —

GUÉRIN. Happily married!

FRANÇOISE. Yes, happily!

GUÉRIN. Dear old Marcel! I'll be so glad to see him!

FRANÇOISE. I see you haven't forgotten my husband, Monsieur. Thank you!

GUÉRIN. How can I help admiring so stout and loyal a heart as his!

FRANÇOISE. You'll have to like me, too!

GUÉRIN. I already do.

FRANÇOISE. Really? Then you believe everything you write?

GUÉRIN. Yes, Madame.

FRANÇOISE. Take care! This morning I was re-reading one of your letters, in which you promised me your heartiest support. [*Holding out her hand to him.*] Then we're friends, are we not?

GUÉRIN [*after hesitating a while, takes her hand in his*]. Good friends, Madame!

FRANÇOISE. Word of honor?

GUÉRIN. Word of honor!

FRANÇOISE [*sitting*]. Then I'll stay. Sit down, and let's talk! [*Guérin is uncertain.*] We have so much to say to each other! Let's talk about you first.

GUÉRIN [*forced to sit down*]. About me? But I —

FRANÇOISE. Yes, about you!

GUÉRIN [*quickly*]. No, about *your* happiness, your welfare —!

FRANÇOISE. About my great happiness!

GUÉRIN [*ironically*]. Let us speak about your — existence — which you are so content with. I must know all the happiness of this house!

FRANÇOISE. Happy people never have anything to say.

GUÉRIN. You never have troubles, I presume?

FRANÇOISE. None, so far.

GUÉRIN. What might happen? To-day you are living peacefully with Marcel, a man whose marriage with you was strongly opposed, it seems. Life owes you no more than it has already given you.

FRANÇOISE. My happiness is complete. I had never imagined that the goodness of a man could make a woman so happy!

GUÉRIN. The goodness —?

FRANÇOISE. Of course!

GUÉRIN. The love, you mean, Madame!

FRANÇOISE. Oh, Marcel's love for me —!

GUÉRIN. Something lacking?

FRANÇOISE. Oh, no!

GUÉRIN [*interested*]. Tell me. Am I not your friend?

FRANÇOISE. Seriously, Monsieur, you know him very well,— how could he possibly be in love with me? Is it even possible? He lets me love him, and I ask nothing more.

GUÉRIN. Nothing?

FRANÇOISE. Only to be allowed to continue to do so. [*Gesture from Guérin.*] I am not at all like other women. I don't ask for rights; but I do demand tenderness and consideration. He is free, I am not — I'll admit that. But I don't mind, I only hope that we may continue as we are!

GUÉRIN. Have you some presentiment, Madame?

FRANÇOISE. I am afraid, Monsieur. My

happiness is not of the proud, demonstrative variety, it is a kind of happiness that is continually trembling for its safety. If I told you —

GUÉRIN. Do tell me!

FRANÇOISE. Later! How I pity one who loves and has to suffer for it!

GUÉRIN [*surprised*]. You —!

FRANÇOISE. I am on the side of the jealous, of the betrayed —

GUÉRIN [*aside, and truly moved to sympathy*]. Poor little woman! [*With great sincerity.*] Then you are not sure of him?

FRANÇOISE [*growing more and more excited*]. He is Marcel! Admit for a moment that he loves me to-day — I want so to believe it! — To-morrow will he love me? Does he himself know whether he will love me then? Isn't he at the mercy of whims, a passing fantasy — of the weather, or the appearance of the first woman he happens to meet? I am only twenty, and I am not always as careful as I might be. Happiness is so difficult!

GUÉRIN. Yes, it is. [*To himself.*] It is! [*To Françoise.*] Perhaps you are conscientious, too sincere?

FRANÇOISE. I feel that; yes, I think I am, but every time I try to hide my affection from him, he becomes indifferent, almost mean — as if he were glad to be rid of some duty — of being good!

GUÉRIN. So it's come to that!

FRANÇOISE. You see, Marcel can't get used to the idea that his other life is over, dead and buried, that he's married for good — that he must do as others do. I do my best and tell him, but my very presence only reminds him of his duties as a husband. For instance [*interrupting herself.*] Here I am telling you all this —

GUÉRIN. Oh! — Please!

FRANÇOISE [*with bitterness*]. He likes to go out alone at night, without me. He knows me well enough to understand that his being away makes me very unhappy, and as a matter of form, of common courtesy, he asks me whether I should like to go with him. I try to reason with myself, and convince myself that he doesn't mean what he says, but I can't help feeling sincerely happy when once in a while I do accept his invitation. But the moment we leave the house I see my mistake. Then he pretends to be in high spirits, but I know all the time he is merely acting a part; and when we come home again he lets drop without fail some hint about his having lost his liberty, that he took me out in a moment of weakness, that he really wanted to be alone.

GUÉRIN [*interrupting.*] And when he does go out alone —?

FRANÇOISE. Then I am most unhappy; I'm in torment for hours and hours. I wonder where he can be, and then I fear he won't come back at all. When the door opens, when I hear him come in, I'm so happy that I pay no attention to what he tells me. But I made a solemn promise with myself never to give the slightest indication of jealousy. My face is always tranquil, and what I say to him never betrays what I feel. I never knowingly betray myself, but his taking way, his tenderness, soon make me confess every fear; then he turns round and using my own confessions as weapons, shows me how wrong I am to be so afraid and suspicious. And when sometimes I say nothing to him, even when he tries to make me confess, he punishes me most severely by telling me stories of his affairs, narrow escapes, and all his temptations. He once told me about an old mistress of his, whom he had just seen, a very clever woman, who was never jealous! Or else he comes in so late that I have to be glad, for if he came in later, it would have been all night! He tells me he had some splendid opportunity, and had to give it up! A thousand things like that! He seems to delight in making me suspect and doubt him!

GUÉRIN. Poor little woman!

FRANÇOISE. That's my life; as for my happiness, it exists from day to day. [*With an air of revolt.*] If I only had the right to be unhappy! But I must always wear a smile, I must be happy, not only in his presence, officially, but to the very depths of my soul! So that he may deceive me without the slightest feeling of remorse! It is his pleasure!

[*She bursts into tears.*]

GUÉRIN [*rising*]. The selfish brute!

FRANÇOISE. Isn't my suffering a reproach to him?

GUÉRIN. I pity you, Madame, and I think I understand you better than any one else. I have trouble not unlike your own; perhaps greater, inconsolable troubles.

FRANÇOISE. If you understand me, Monsieur, advise me. I need you!

GUÉRIN [*startled back into reality*]. Me, your aid? I? [*Aside.*] No!

FRANÇOISE. You spoke of your friendship. The time has come, prove that it is real!

GUÉRIN. Madame, why did I ever see you? Why did I listen to you?

FRANÇOISE. What have you to regret?

GUÉRIN. Nothing, Madame, nothing.

FRANÇOISE. Explain yourself, Monsieur. You — you make me afraid!

GUÉRIN [*trying to calm her suspicions*]. Don't cry like that! There is nothing to behave that way about! Your husband doesn't love you as he ought, but he does love you. You are jealous, that's what's troubling you. And for that matter, why should he deceive you? That would be too unjust —

FRANÇOISE [*excited*]. Too unjust! You are right, Monsieur! No matter how cynical, how blasé a man may be, isn't it his duty, his sacred duty to say to himself, " I have found a good and true woman in this world of deception; she is a woman who adores me, who is only too ready to invent any excuse for me! She bears my name and honors it; no matter what I do, she is always true, of that I am positive. I am always foremost in her thoughts, and I shall be her only love." When a man can say all that, Monsieur, isn't that real, true happiness?

GUÉRIN [*sobbing*]. Yes — that is happiness!

FRANÇOISE. You are crying! [*A pause.*]

GUÉRIN. My wife — deceived me!

FRANÇOISE. Oh! — [*A pause.*] Marcel —

GUÉRIN. Your happiness is in no danger!

Yesterday I found some old letters, in a desk — old letters — that was all! You weren't his wife at the time. It's all ancient history.

FRANÇOISE [*aside*]. Who knows?

GUÉRIN. Forgive me, Madame; your troubles make me think of my own. When you told of the happiness you can still give, I couldn't help thinking of what I had lost!

FRANÇOISE. So you have come to get my husband to fight a duel with you?

GUÉRIN. Madame —

FRANÇOISE. You are going to fight him? Answer me.

GUÉRIN. My life is a wreck now — I must —

FRANÇOISE. I don't ask you to forget; Monsieur —

GUÉRIN. Don't you think I have a right —?

FRANÇOISE. Stop!

GUÉRIN. No, then; I shall not try to kill him. You love him too much! I couldn't do it now! In striking him I should be injuring you, and you don't deserve to suffer; you have betrayed no one! The happiness you have just taught me to know is as sacred and inviolable as my honor, my unhappiness. I shall not seek revenge.

FRANÇOISE [*gratefully*]. Oh, Monsieur.

GUÉRIN. I am willing he should live, because he is so dear, so necessary to you. Keep him. If he wants to spoil your happiness, his be the blame! I shall not do it! It would be sacrilege! Good-by, Madame, good-by.

[*Guérin goes out, back, Françoise falls into a chair, sobbing.*]

[*Enter Marcel by the little door.*]

MARCEL [*aside, with a melancholy air*]. Refused to see me!

FRANÇOISE [*distantly*]. Oh, it's you!

MARCEL [*good-humoredly*]. Yes, it's I. [*A pause. He goes toward her.*] You have been crying! Have you seen Guérin? He's been here!

FRANÇOISE. Marcel —

MARCEL. Did he dare tell you —!

FRANÇOISE. You won't see any more of him.

MARCEL [*astounded*]. He's not going to fight?

FRANÇOISE. He refuses.

MARCEL. Thank you!

FRANÇOISE. I took good care of your dignity, you may be sure of that. Here we were together; I told him the story of my life during the last year — how I loved you — and then he broke down.— When I learned the truth, he said he would go away for the sake of my happiness.

MARCEL. I was a coward to deceive that man! — Is this a final sentence that you pass on me?

FRANÇOISE. Marcel!

MARCEL. Both of you are big! You have big hearts! I admire you both more than I can say.

FRANÇOISE [*incredulously*]. Where are you going? To get him to fight with you?

MARCEL [*returning to her; angrily*]. How can I, now? After what you have done, it would be absurd. Why the devil did you have to mix yourself up in something that didn't concern you? I was only looking for a chance to fight that duel!

FRANÇOISE. Looking for a chance?

MARCEL. Oh, I —

FRANÇOISE. Why?

MARCEL [*between his teeth*]. That's my affair! Everybody has his enemies — his insults to avenge. It was a very good thing that that gentleman didn't happen across my path!

FRANÇOISE. How can you dare to recall what he has been generous enough to forget?

MARCEL. How do you know that I haven't a special reason for fighting this duel? A legitimate reason, that must be concealed from you?

FRANÇOISE. You are mistaken, dear: I guess that reason perfectly.

MARCEL. Really?

FRANÇOISE. I know it.

MARCEL [*bursting forth*]. Oh! Good!! You haven't always been so frightfully profound!

FRANÇOISE. Yes, I have, and your irony only proves that I have not been so much mistaken in what I have felt by intuition.

MARCEL. Ah, marriage!

FRANÇOISE. Ah, duty!

MARCEL. I love Madame Guérin, don't I?

FRANÇOISE. I don't say that.

MARCEL. You think it.

FRANÇOISE. And if I do? Would it be a crime to think it? You once loved her — perhaps you have seen her again, not very long ago. Do I know where you go? You never tell me.

MARCEL. I tell you too much!

FRANÇOISE. I think you do.

MARCEL. You're jealous!

FRANÇOISE. Common, if you like. Come, you must admit, Marcel, Madame Guérin has something to do with your excitement now?

MARCEL. Very well then, I love her, I adore her! Are you satisfied now?

FRANÇOISE. You should have told me that at first, my dear; I should never have tried to keep you away from her.

[*She breaks into tears.*]

MARCEL. She's crying! God, there's my liberty!

FRANÇOISE [*bitterly*]. Your liberty? I did not suffer when I promised you your liberty.

MARCEL. That was your "resignation"!

FRANÇOISE. You knew life, I did not. You ought never to have accepted it!

MARCEL. You're like all the rest!

FRANÇOISE [*more excited*]. Doesn't unhappiness level us all?

MARCEL. I see it does!

FRANÇOISE. What can you ask for them? So long as you have no great happiness like mine you are ready enough to make any sacrifice, but when once you have it, you never resign yourself to losing it.

MARCEL. That's just the difficulty.

FRANÇOISE. Be a little patient, dear: I have not yet reached that state of cynicism and subtlety which you seem to want in your wife — I thought I came near to your ideal once! Perhaps there's some hope for me yet: I have promised myself that I should do my best to satisfy your ideal.

MARCEL [*moved*]. I don't ask that.

FRANÇOISE. You are right, I am very foolish to try to struggle. What will be the good? It will suffice when I have lost the dearest creature to me on earth — through my foolishness, my blunders!

MARCEL. The dearest creature —?

FRANÇOISE. I can't help it if he seems so to me!

MARCEL [*disarmed*]. You — you're trying to appeal to my vanity!

FRANÇOISE. I am hardly in the mood for joking.

MARCEL [*tenderly, as he falls at her feet*]. But you make me say things like that — I don't know what —! I am not bad — really bad! No, I have not deceived you! I love you, and only you! You!! You know that, Françoise! Ask — ask any woman!! All women!

[*A pause.*]

FRANÇOISE [*smiling through her tears*]. Best of husbands! You're not going out then? You'll stay?

MARCEL [*in Françoise's arms*]. Can I go now, now that I'm here? You are so pretty that I —

FRANÇOISE. Not when I'm in trouble.

MARCEL. Don't cry!

FRANÇOISE. I forgive you!

MARCEL. Wait, I haven't confessed everything.

FRANÇOISE. Not another word!

MARCEL. I want to be sincere!

FRANÇOISE. I prefer to have you lie to me!

MARCEL. First, read this telegram — the one I received this morning.

FRANÇOISE [*surprised*]. From Madame Guérin?

MARCEL. You saw her not long ago. Yes, she calmly told me —

FRANÇOISE. That her husband had found some letters!

MARCEL. And that she was about to leave for England with her lover.

FRANÇOISE. Then she is quite consoled?

MARCEL. Perfectly.

FRANÇOISE. Poor Marcel! And you went to see her and try to prevent her going away with him?

MARCEL. My foolishness was well punished. She wouldn't receive me.

FRANÇOISE. Then I am the only one left who loves you? How happy I am!

MARCEL. I'll kill that love some day with my ridiculous affairs!

FRANÇOISE [*gravely*]. I defy you!

MARCEL [*playfully*]. Then I no longer have the right to provoke Monsieur Guérin? Now?

FRANÇOISE [*gaily*]. You are growing old, Lovelace, his wife has deceived you!

MARCEL [*lovingly*]. Françoise' luck! [*Sadly.*] Married!

[CURTAIN.]

The Dupe

(*La Dupe*)

A Comedy in Five Acts

By

GEORGES ANCEY

TRANSLATED BY

BARRETT H. CLARK

Produced for the first time, at the Théâtre Libre, 21 December, 1891.

PERSONS REPRESENTED:

ORIGINAL CAST

ALBERT	M. Antoine
MADAME VIOT	Mlles. Barny
ADÈLE	Henriot
MARIE	Dulac

The scene is the drawing-room in an apartment at Paris. The time is the present.

THE DUPE

ACT I

[*Mme. Viot and Marie are on the stage as the curtain rises.*]

MME. VIOT. And what if she is unwilling? You know she is hard to handle.

MARIE. If she is unwilling, then she must be severely talked to. She's refused five or six very favorable chances! And now here is this nice-looking, wealthy young man of good family — it would be very, very foolish to let him escape — perhaps very imprudent. Adèle has 300,000 francs' dowry, I know, but she's twenty-three already; it's time she was married!

MME. VIOT. My dear child, you are absolutely right.

MARIE. You must admit that when it was a question of finding me a husband I didn't give you so much trouble.

MME. VIOT. You certainly didn't. You behaved beautifully!

MARIE. And yet, it isn't very hard to see that you prefer my sister to me. You don't dare scold her.

MME. VIOT. I? Oh, Marie, I do everything for you! Your father always used to say to me: "Madame Viot," he said, "you love Marie better than Adèle." Only the other day, in that business about the will —

MARIE. You're not going to blame me — ?

MME. VIOT. No, you dear child, and I'm only too happy when I can do something for you. I do everything in my power, and sometimes I'm even unjust to Adèle. I know she wouldn't like the way I favored you, and if she knew that the day I die —

MARIE. Don't talk about it! But then, you see, Adèle doesn't care about those things: money is nothing to her. You have no reason to feel sorry for her.

MME. VIOT. I don't. Now what shall I say to Adèle?

MARIE. *I* don't know, you can think of something. Tell her, for instance, that M. Bonnet is really a wonderful match. Then add that you desire nothing better than her happiness, that that is your sole reason for existence — tell her your love for her! We always say that to children when we want them to do something.

MME. VIOT. Good. I'll follow your advice, as I always do. You have so much common sense — you see things so clearly!

MARIE. Only remember not to drag me in; I love Adèle immensely. I don't want any of the responsibility in this affair.

MME. VIOT. Well, you were the first, after all, to mention this possible marriage, and persuaded me to do what I've done. It must succeed! But not long ago —

MARIE. Oh, Mama, you're quite mistaken. I simply advised you to consider M. Bonnet. You know, he's acquainted with my husband; his family may be able to help Gustave a little in a business way. I said this marriage would be a good stroke for us all. I said that it had to be. Outside that, I had nothing to do with the case. I always wanted to remain neutral, and neutral shall I remain. I know nothing, and I don't want to know anything. And to prove it, I again advise you to act according to your own ideas. Above all, don't imagine that I waited until you had already decided! — For you *have* decided, haven't you? —

MME. VIOT. Yes —

MARIE. No, I don't want to know! Now, think well; it will be a big responsibility on your part — giving Adèle a husband she doesn't care for. Look well into it all, and forget me: I don't count. Adèle is the only one who really counts. Dear Adèle! If I were you, I'd hesitate a long time.— M. Bonnet —! M. Bonnet —!

MME. VIOT. Of course, you're not forcing me to decide! But really I want it. It is a necessity. I want it in spite of you.

MARIE. Mama, there is only one thing I really care about on earth: that you should love us both. I believe that my sole reason for existing is for your sake.

MME. VIOT. Dear child!

MARIE. Come now. Tell Adèle to come here. Tell her, too, all I told you to tell her.

MME. VIOT [*calling*]— Adèle —!

[*Enter Adèle.*]

[*To Adèle.*] Look at me — your face — Yes, you look nice. Fix your curls, there! Turn round. Good.

MARIE. Charming.

ADÈLE. What's this, Mama?

MME. VIOT. You ought to know. M. Bonnet, whom you've seen once or twice, has asked for your hand in marriage. He's coming, and you're to give us all your answer.

ADÈLE. Who is this M. Bonnet?

MME. VIOT. You know very well: that young man who danced with you at the Marcellins'.

ADÈLE. I don't remember him.

MME. VIOT. No matter. Only keep this one thing well in mind: my heart is set on this marriage, which will be of great advantage to us all. Just remember that, and be as nice as you can to him. He's coming to make us a visit, just as if it were an ordinary call. Talk with him, and behave sensibly.

ADÈLE. Very well, Mama.

MARIE. Dear sister!

MME. VIOT. There's the bell! It's he! Oh, his name is Albert.

[*Enter Albert Bonnet.*]

Ah, M. Bonnet! Adèle, bring a chair — I hope you are well, Monsieur?

ALBERT. Very well, Madame, and you? — [*To Marie.*] How are you, Madame? Is M. Chesneau well?

MARIE. Perfectly, thank you.

ALBERT. Mademoiselle!

ADÈLE. Monsieur!

ALBERT. I beg your pardon, Madame, for

coming so early, but I'm so busy now; I have a great many important and pressing matters on hand — I can scarcely find an hour to myself all day long. But I so wanted to thank you for the invitation you sent me not long ago for that dance at the Marcellins', and I thought I should take advantage of a leisure moment — and perform a — duty — which is at the same time — a — pleasure — yes, indeed — a — pleasure. I have no hesitation in employing that expression; it is even a trifle feeble to express what I feel. It falls far short of the truth — I assure you. For — with the exception of M. Chesneau, I have the good fortune of finding all the family together.

MME. VIOT. Too good of you! We are really delighted to see you!

MARIE. Certainly! [*To Adèle.*] Say something!

ADÈLE [*to Marie*]. What? [*A pause.*]

MME. VIOT. And — Your father is quite well?

ALBERT. Yes, Madame, fortunately — in spite of this extraordinary cold weather. I wonder if it will continue?

MME. VIOT. Oh, we certainly hope not.

MARIE. A little rain will doubtless bring milder weather.

ALBERT. But it's very disagreeable now; streets dirty, sidewalks all slushy — are they not, Mademoiselle?

ADÈLE. Oh, of course, Monsieur! [*They laugh. A pause.*]

MME. VIOT. And — your mother is in good health?

ALBERT. Oh, always about the same. We don't dare hope to have her with us much longer.

MARIE. Really? [*A pause.*]

MME. VIOT. And your uncle is not too troubled with his gout?

ALBERT. I'm afraid he is. This weather, you know —!

MME. VIOT. Fortunately, your aunt is able to take good care of him. What a splendid woman your aunt is!

ALBERT. Oh, yes. [*A pause.*]

MARIE. Our family is very lucky. Not one of us troubled with gout. We all have fine constitutions: my mother, myself, my sister — haven't you, Adèle?

ADÈLE. Oh, yes, I'm always well. [*They laugh again.*]

ALBERT. I see, Mademoiselle has delicious coloring — usually the sign of a robust constitution.

MME. VIOT. She is a great favorite with us, as well she might be. I can truly say that she has been well brought up according to all the good principles of the family. You know, she speaks three languages, almost as well as her mother-tongue: English, Italian, and — and — German. German is so difficult, you know —!

MARIE. I never could learn it!

ALBERT. A splendid thing, if Mademoiselle ever marries a business man. We find very few people in our employ who know that language.

MME. VIOT. Indeed! And then, she plays

the piano very nicely. Won't you play us a little something, and show M. Albert — ?

ALBERT. Ah, Mademoiselle, if you would be so good! I hardly dared ask —

ADÈLE. You are too good, Monsieur, but I really don't know anything to play. [*She giggles.*]

MME. VIOT. We mustn't torment her. But her favorite art, the one in which she shows most talent, is painting —

MARIE. My sister does some very good porcelain work.

ALBERT. Really? Might I see something — ?

MME. VIOT. Dearie, show Monsieur that plate you are just finishing.

ALBERT. I beg you!

ADÈLE [*who has gone to get the plate*]. Here!

ALBERT. How pretty, how pretty!

MME. VIOT. Not half bad!

ALBERT. That little Cupid, up there — !

MME. VIOT. You might almost think it was going to fly away!

ALBERT. And he does, Madame — he does, — very ingenious! — He's flying to pluck a rose! So poetic! So graceful!

MME. VIOT. Yes, she's a very fair amateur.

ALBERT. Amateur? This is not the work of an amateur, Madame. This is the work of an artist!

MARIE. Isn't sister going to exhibit it at the Salon?

ALBERT. I was just going to suggest that!

MME. VIOT. You are too good!

ALBERT. I say merely what I think. You know, I felt all along, before I came here, that Mademoiselle was different from other young ladies — the kind you meet at social gatherings. We danced together at the Marcellins'— only too little, for Mademoiselle Adèle dances perfectly. We spoke about travel, did we not?

ADÈLE. Yes, I remember. [*She laughs again.*]

ALBERT. That affair was very delightful. And I can say, without appearing to exaggerate, that your presence there went far to make it so. Mademoiselle Adèle is so charming, so amiable, so refined, so — let us be frank — so pretty, that to her alone was due the pleasure of that soirée. What cleverness, and good sense! And her power of expressing things, her manner of speech and carriage! And that air of distinction — gets it from her family — Mademoiselle comes of good stock, assuredly! Distinction is a *rara avis* in these days, too. It is all the more charming in Mademoiselle, as it is allied with a wonderfully equal temper and good humor —

MME. VIOT. Monsieur —!

ALBERT. Of course! I repeat: distinction of bearing, in her manner of dressing. Mlle. Adèle is perfection in everything! As for myself, Madame, I have occasion to meet many people in society, and for as long as I can remember, I have never met, among all the young ladies with whom I have danced, a single one with the charming simplicity of Mademoiselle.— But, I beg you, stop me — I shall never end this talk. And yet: one word more. It's about that pretty dress she wore that evening at the Marcellins'.

MME. VIOT. Do you notice such things, then?

ALBERT. I should think so! And how well she wore it! There are so many people who haven't the slightest idea how to wear clothes. The same criticism certainly cannot be made in her case; I shall never forget that pink dress —

MME. VIOT. It wasn't pink!

ALBERT. Of course! I was confusing it with that of the lady next to her. It was blue!

MME. VIOT. No — gray!

ALBERT. Yes, gray! In the artificial light, you know —!

[*A pause of embarrassment.*]

MARIE. It's only natural, you know, that we should be well dressed: we have a first-rate modiste.

ALBERT. Oh, the modiste isn't everything. [*They laugh.*] Well, now, I must be going, Madame. I am very sorry to have to leave you so abruptly, but business is business! I have an important engagement. Madame! Madame! Mademoiselle! [*Albert goes out.*]

MME. VIOT [*to Marie*]. Charming, isn't he?

MARIE. Not half bad.

MME. VIOT [*to Adèle*]. What do you think?

ADÈLE. Well, Mama, M. Bonnet —

MME. VIOT. Well, what? M. Bonnet —? Can't you say something else?

ADÈLE [*bursting into tears*]. I — I don't like him.

MME. VIOT. There you are crying!

ADÈLE. Please, please, Mama, not that man! I haven't even talked with him, I have hardly seen him —

MME. VIOT. It is not necessary to talk with a young man before you're engaged to him.

ADÈLE. That may be, but I don't love him. There's something about him that revolts me. He's not at all good-looking, and he's nearly bald —

MME. VIOT. Well, if you're so particular about those things —!

ADÈLE. Remember what you used to say to me: to be happy in marriage you must have a husband you love and who loves you.

MME. VIOT. Who says M. Bonnet doesn't love you? If he wants to marry you, you must be attractive to him!

ADÈLE. Or else I must be a good business proposition!

MME. VIOT. Who taught you to reason like that? You're talking nonsense. At your age —!

MARIE. Mama, Mama, the poor dear child!

ADÈLE. You needn't think I've arrived at the age of twenty-three without doing some thinking. I have noticed so many of my girl friends and their marriages —

MARIE [*to Mme. Viot*]. Insist!

MME. VIOT. You've been very badly brought up, that's all. Now, about M. Bonnet: you know your confessor recommended him strongly. And when the Abbé Porel says something, you can take his word for it.

MARIE [*to Adèle*]. Do you mean to say he doesn't know what he's talking about?

MME. VIOT. And think how well he knows you! He baptized you, was with you when you went to First Communion, and helped you with your Catechism. It would be very strange if he didn't know you through and through. He told me that you and M. Bonnet were made for one another, and after making inquiries about him, I agree with the Abbè. M. Bonnet is thirty, he is very charming, a good business man, intelligent, and religious. He is the director of a fire insurance company, *The Central,* I believe. He is very easy to get along with. If you go about it carefully, you can lead him by the nose. He brings a very neat little dowry, and has great promise for the future. You might look a long time to find a better family than his: his father was a judge, and his mother has a brother whose wife is the daughter of a judge of the Commercial Tribunal; the maternal grandfather of M. Bonnet's father was the second husband of the daughter by his second marriage of the celebrated lawyer, Rigault. They are a splendid family: amiable, gracious, and well educated. The other day I was talking with M. Bonnet, your future great-uncle. I never saw so delightful a man. He talked for a whole hour — I couldn't get a word in edgewise.— Well, I have set my heart on this marriage, because it is certain to make a number of very pleasant connections for every one of us. So, we are agreed, aren't we?

MARIE [*to her mother*]. Good!

ADÈLE. But I don't love M. Bonnet!

MARIE. Poor child!

MME. VIOT. A nice answer! When you get

a good chance you must take it. Love comes afterward.

ADÈLE. But I have everything I need right here, Mama. I am perfectly happy as I am. I'd be willing never to marry, if I could always be with you!

MME. VIOT. And never marry?!

ADÈLE. I'm happy. I do as I like. Why not wait, then? I can't bear the thought of leaving my home, and you — all that I've loved. To think of leaving — my own room, that I've fixed up so prettily! That may all seem foolish to you, but I'm — sentimental — you yourself say I am! When you live a long while in one place, you get to love it, and when the time comes to leave, you feel that you're leaving part of yourself there! I'd regret even our little walks together, and our visits. I didn't mind if they were a little tiresome. I'd feel very, very sorry not to hear old Rosalie scold me in the morning, telling me it was time to get up.

MME. VIOT. But you see, as soon as you marry, I've decided to move. I'm going to let you have this apartment and all the furniture. I'm going to live opposite here, just above your sister.

ADÈLE. That isn't the same thing at all!

MARIE. How affectionate of her!

MME. VIOT. Now stop this childishness! I'm getting old, my dear. You can never tell who's going to die and who's going to live on. I don't want to risk not doing all my duty before I go — my whole duty. To look after a little girl of your age is a great responsibility, and I want to get rid of it. You may think it's easy watching you from day to day! I'm losing what little leisure time I have to myself before I die. We have to see you around in society, inquire about all the young men you dance with! I'm thoroughly tired of the whole business! Always on the lookout for a husband for you. Advice, gossip, everywhere — all your friends want you to marry! I'm tired too of getting all dressed up two and three times a week, climbing into a carriage late at night, and sitting out long dances, and coming home, sick and tired, at six in the morning!

ADÈLE. Oh, Mama, we're never later than one!

MME. VIOT. What?

ADÈLE. Never.

MME. VIOT. At any rate, I'm ready to move now. The landlord is increasing the rent; our lease expires in April. In our new apartment there'll be no room for you. If you aren't married by the last of March — at the latest — here I'll be with an apartment beyond my means on my hands. And it'll be your fault if I have to pay a hundred francs a term extra!

ADÈLE. You can afford it ten times over.

MME. VIOT. No, I can't afford it. And I don't want you to say I can. I'd arranged to fix up the new place and at last begin to economize. Not long ago I saw a nice parlor set of furniture that would fit in beautifully — red plush —

ADÈLE. How ugly!

MME. VIOT. Perhaps it is, but it's cheap. Now run along. Here's another bargain I'm going to lose, and it's your fault. Funny — you really are a bother! After all I've done for you, I expected you would be a little nice to me, more devoted —!

ADÈLE. But, I —

MARIE [*to her mother*]. Come to the point.

MME. VIOT [*violently*]. I'm done with you! I shan't argue another minute. You are going to marry —

ADÈLE. Mama!

MME. VIOT. You are going to marry him! You'll thank me afterward. Don't say another word, now — if you're going to cry, go and cry in your own room. We know better than you what sort of husband you need.— The idea!

MARIE. Poor dear!

ADÈLE [*aside to Marie*]. Thank you for defending me!

MARIE. I understand how you feel! [*Adèle goes out.*]

MME. VIOT. Thank you for helping me!

MARIE. You were perfectly right.

MME. VIOT. Well, that's over. What a stubborn child she is! How different you girls are! You're so good!

MARIE. Remember whom I'm named after: the Virgin Mary!

MME. VIOT. You're worthy the name.

MARIE. Let's hope the marriage will be a happy one!

MME. VIOT. No matter what happens, I know I have done my duty!

[CURTAIN.]

ACT II

[*The scene is the same. Adèle and Albert are on the stage as the curtain rises.*]

ADÈLE. Then you're going out?

ALBERT. Yes, sweetheart, I must go to the office.

ADÈLE. Just five minutes more! That's a nice sort of office to have, where you must go at night! Just five minutes, dear.

ALBERT. Well, five minutes — no longer.

ADÈLE. You good boy! Sit down there now, and don't move, while I have a good long look at you.

ALBERT. Child! You might think we were married only yesterday!

ADÈLE. Dearest, we haven't been for so long, you know —! Hardly a year. We can still love each other and not seem foolish, can't we?

ALBERT. Certainly, certainly.

ADÈLE. And I do love you — how I love you! — funny, isn't it?

ALBERT. Funny? That you love me?

ADÈLE. Yes.

ALBERT. I think you are a little — off?

ADÈLE. That's what you can't understand — you don't know — [*She laughs.*]

ALBERT. Why —!

ADÈLE. You're so ridiculous when you're surprised. Look that way again — once more, please! Now I'll tell you everything.

ALBERT. Tell me —

ADÈLE. It's funny that I love you now, because I didn't use to —

ALBERT. When?

ADÈLE. Before we were married — I couldn't see anything in you.

ALBERT. Indeed?

ADÈLE. Are you angry?

ALBERT. Of course not!

ADÈLE. I'll never forget the day you came to pay a visit to Mama, and meet me. How I nearly died laughing to myself — and crying, too, because I knew well enough that I had to marry you.— You don't hold that against me, do you?

ALBERT. Not in the least — I think it's very amusing.

ADÈLE. You made an awful impression on me, with your bald head — oh, awful! Then you seemed so embarrassed with that gold-headed cane of yours! And what a time you had making compliments to me! And what compliments they were! "Mademoiselle, you paint superbly! — Mademoiselle, you dance beautifully!" And my dress, the one I wore to the Marcellins', the one you perfectly remembered! And Mama asked you what color it was, and then you forgot! What a slip! How you amused me, and how I laughed! Your answering that it was pink, and then blue! Right now, I'll wager you don't know what color it was! Just tell me, and let's see!

ALBERT. Well, it *was* blue!

ADÈLE [*laughing loudly*]. No! Gray! Maker of compliments whether they're true or not!

ALBERT. Of course, it was gray.

ADÈLE. Now you remember. Gray, gray, gray!

ALBERT. Of course.

ADÈLE. Then after that great success of yours, you thought it was time you put an end to your visit, you imagined I had had sufficient opportunity to observe your charms, your conversational qualities. Then you got up, looking as though you were afraid that perhaps you hadn't been quite as brilliant as you had hoped to be. And then you left, very ceremoniously. My dear, if you thought for one instant that that day, when you put your gold-headed cane in the umbrella-rack, you had made the conquest of my affections, you were mistaken. Just after you went, Mama told me I was to marry you, so that she could move at once. Here she had to pay too much rent! What a reason!

ALBERT. Your mother is a funny one!

ADÈLE. Then I cried — cried like a Magdalen! I even kept it up till the day of my marriage; even after, I had to have a little time to become accustomed, to console myself.

ALBERT. But now you love me?

ADÈLE. Do I?!

ALBERT. And how did it happen?

ADÈLE. One evening, last summer, at Mama's, in the country. It was four months after our marriage. Up to that time, I was in a whirlpool of thoughts and sensations — I couldn't really collect myself. The first days, I didn't know where I was: I was angry, all cut up — I must have seemed queer to you? But I couldn't help it. Everything seemed so new and so disgusting. Yet one evening, you said something to me, and it kept ringing in my ears. It seems perhaps very commonplace, but you called me "Dearest," — so nicely, so sweetly, that — well — I can't explain! Then Mama and I left for the country, where you came nearly every night, from Paris. Then I felt so queer: when you were there I wished you were a long way off; when you were away, I wanted you near me.— Ask Mama, her room was next to mine there. [*Laughing.*] She'll tell you that I called for you in the night! When we talked together, your voice sounded strange. There were moments when your voice breaking the silence, made me feel faint. And always the thought of your "Dearest"! It was like a caress! At last, one June night, we took a long walk in the park. The window of our room had been open all day, it was filled with the sweet perfume of the fields. How sweet it was! I was quite intoxicated! And I kept talking and talking, and you kissed me to make me stop! You took me in your arms, rudely, like my master. Then I was afraid of nothing. From then on, I had no more fear, no more misgivings. I was your slave. I love you, I adore you! Kiss me, Albert! And — don't go to the office to-night!

ALBERT. The little child! Come now, no foolishness! I must go —

ADÈLE. Is it so important —?

ALBERT. A very pressing business matter. A great deal depends on the result.

ADÈLE. Go then, and come back quickly.

ALBERT. I'll go and come back immediately — in fifteen minutes.

ADÈLE. You *are* going to your office, aren't you?

ALBERT. Where else should I go? Are you jealous?

ADÈLE [*laughing*]. I was only fooling. Good-by!

ALBERT. I'll come back soon. Good-by. [*He goes out.*]

ADÈLE. I love him! [*After a pause.*] I wonder if it's true what he said the other day, that a woman should not love her husband too blindly, that if she is really sensible and considerate, she should be reserved, so that she can keep him well in hand? To be a superior and intelligent wife? Do like my sister? Every moment be on the alert to look after your husband's welfare, and in that way, get "around" him? If you don't do that, he will get the better of you — Then marriage is a struggle, where either the husband or the wife must be the victor. The people who say that have never loved! No, I won't follow their advice! I can't do it! It's too sweet to let yourself be domineered over. I know I'm only a little foolish wife.— Oh, here comes Marie!

[*Enter Marie.*]

MARIE. How nice it is to live so near! My husband has gone to bed, and I thought I'd run over to see you a moment.

ADÈLE. Your husband in bed so soon? At this hour? Is he sick?

MARIE. No, it's only a habit of his.

ADÈLE [*smiling*]. That you persuade him to keep up!

MARIE. What?

ADÈLE. Nothing. You must forgive me if I sound foolish: I'm so happy! I think parents are quite right in forcing their daughters to marry. When girls are young, they have no sense. Dear Albert!

MARIE. Is dear Albert here?

ADÈLE. No, he's just gone to the office. He'll be back at ten.

MARIE. Oh, he goes out evenings, now?

ADÈLE. Just to the office!

MARIE. It's dangerous; even to the office!

ADÈLE. You are too suspicious: I'm perfectly sure of him. Of course, it's natural, you know: some people are confiding, and others not. A man must have some freedom. I should never love a man who would do everything I liked. It's nice once in a while to be refused.

MARIE. Think so?

ADÈLE. Yes — rather — or — well, I hardly know. Just now I'm a little mad, I'm so happy!

MARIE. Yet I advise you to refuse to let him go out at night, no matter how good his excuse is. This going to theaters, and cafés and clubs — clubs above all —!

ADÈLE. But *we* love each other! [*A pause.*]

MARIE. I was at Mme. Rousseau's to-day.

ADÈLE. Indeed?

MARIE. Yes.

ADÈLE. What did the good Mme. Rousseau tell you?

MARIE. A thousand things.

ADÈLE. Secrets?

MARIE. Oh, not at all! She asked about you, and then talked about your husband.

ADÈLE. Did she?

MARIE. What a singular woman she is. It seems that she is always meddling with something that doesn't concern her.

ADÈLE. She certainly is!

MARIE. Of course, she seems to be very well informed. She says some things that are not in the least pleasant to hear.

ADÈLE. Did she tell you anything like that about Albert?

MARIE. No, no, not about your husband —

ADÈLE. Really? You look rather queer —

MARIE. Of course not —

ADÈLE [*leaving her work*]. I love Albert so deeply that the slightest suspicion upsets me terribly.

MARIE. Poor little dear! You're a perfect darling! If he ever thought of being unfaithful to you, he'd be the lowest of blackguards! But you have no cause for worry —

ADÈLE. I'm not anxious.

MARIE. And you're right.— [*A pause.*] Proofs, real proofs are what are always needed in time of danger.

ADÈLE. I know that Mme. Rousseau said something about my husband.

MARIE. But it was all so foolish!

ADÈLE. Well, what did she say?

MARIE. Lies, of course. I ask you, how *could* Albert, who loves you, have married you to pay off his debts, and now keep his former mistress, a woman of forty?

ADÈLE. Did she say that?

MARIE. Yes.

ADÈLE. Let her then, I don't care! It's just funny, that's all.

MARIE. But that isn't all. Just imagine, she says your husband was surprised with this woman in his arms —

ADÈLE. By whom?

MARIE. By M. and Mme. Rousseau.

ADÈLE. And what did M. Rousseau say? As a rule, he is not inclined to treat things lightly.

MARIE. He corroborates his wife, and adds something.

ADÈLE. What?

MARIE. He declares that Albert has rented an apartment for this woman not far from here, in order to be near her. He even knows the lady's name: Caroline — yes, I think that's it! What gossiping scandal-mongers there are in this world!

ADÈLE. Caroline? Caroline?

MARIE. What's the matter with you?

ADÈLE. I seem to remember something, myself. Something seemed peculiar, but I believed Albert's explanations. Could it be true, then? Are the Rousseaus right? One day, Albert was at the office, I saw a letter that had come for him — it was in his desk — it was from a woman — signed "Caroline." I showed it to him, but he swore that was ancient history. He seemed very much surprised to see it; "That should have been burned long ago," he said. He then told me that he had never had anything to do with her. He even laughed at what had happened, and I remember that I laughed with him. Yet I remember that the letter must have been written quite recently: the ink seemed fresh. Where *is* that letter? I'll show it to you. We must get to the bottom of this now.— Where did I put it? It began with "My Dear Albert"— Now I can't find it! — And to think that another woman has called him "My Dear Albert"! Where is it?

MARIE. Don't bother so much about a little gossip. There's really nothing the matter! Don't cry about it — I can't bear to see you cry!

ADÈLE. You're right: it's nothing at all. I know Albert would not deceive me. The whole thing's only a story made up by disagreeable people. If you only knew how nice Albert is! Just now, when we were talking together, he was so open and frank! Could he have been thinking of some one else at such a time? Could he deceive me? Nonsense! [*Suddenly taking fright.*] And yet —

MARIE. Yet?

ADÈLE. It's rather strange how certain things come to mind at times! — Only the other day — I never thought of it before, yet it's clear now! — Shall I always be thinking of something evil? No, no, no — and yet —? It's this: the other day, I walked half-way to his office with him. We got to the end of the Palais Royal garden — under the little archway where there aren't any shops, at the foot of the little stairway leading to the Rue Vivienne, we passed a light-complexioned woman, rather tall — she was smiling — as if she were meeting a friend. I looked at my husband. Funny, he was smiling, too. I remember perfectly: then he kept on smiling at her. How foolish I am! It's only my imagination, I know! What if he did smile at her? Perhaps — well — and if he did? Perhaps he didn't know her? As any one might. But then people don't do it — that way! Then something else! As soon as we'd go up the stairs, I left him. I had an errand to do. As I was leaving, I saw him go back; instead of going to the Bourse, he went the other way! To join that woman we passed!

MARIE. He may have gone to see his friend Berard, who lives in the Rue Montpensier?

ADÈLE. An old friend — yes, possibly — probably — But no! Then he would have gone to the left. He didn't, he went after that woman who had come down the stairs.— How awful! He *is* deceiving me! I know it! And I loved him so! — What a fool I've been! There wasn't a day I didn't think of it, look forward to the time he'd be coming back from the office, to our little dinner all to ourselves, and the evenings we'd spend together. I was so happy, so confident! — What a life I have before me! — I never deserved this blow!

MARIE. My dear Adèle! Don't go on that way! If I had known all this was going to happen, I should never have repeated what I heard! Now be brave. You really have no proofs, you know. How do you know you're not the victim of an awful lie? Ask your husband, be very careful how — then you'll have time to decide what you want to do.

ADÈLE. You're right — I must first be positive — I must know. Perhaps I am jumping at conclusions.— Sh! There's his key in the lock! I'll speak to him.

MARIE. My dear Adèle, be calm, though.— I'll leave you alone with him. Courage, now! — Oh, if I'd only known before! What a fool I am! Will you forgive me? After all, I've only done my duty as a sister.

[*Enter Albert.*]

ALBERT. You here? [*To Adèle.*] I'm very sorry: I was kept — couldn't help it — met a friend —

MARIE. I'm going — I must get to bed. Eleven o'clock! It's high time!

ALBERT. Eleven! That's right. I've been a whole hour!

MARIE. Good night. Poor dear! How I blame myself!

[*She goes out.*]

ALBERT. I really don't like coming in so late. — Old friend got hold of me in the street, and simply wouldn't let me go. I simply couldn't get away.

ADÈLE. Albert!

ALBERT. Yes?

ADÈLE. Look me in the eyes! — You're deceiving me!

ALBERT. Why —!

ADÈLE. You're deceiving me!

ALBERT. Adèle, this is ridiculous —

ADÈLE. Swear that you're not —!

ALBERT [*embarrassed*]. If you want me to — of course I swear —

ADÈLE. How absurd of me to ask you! I have only to look at you to see where you've been!

ALBERT. Why, what's the matter?

ADÈLE [*snatching off his collar and tie*]. You're not even dressed! This collar isn't fastened! The tie is not tied —

ALBERT. It was so warm in the street!

ADÈLE. Not in the street! Deny it if you can!

ALBERT. Well, then, I don't! And be damned to you!

ADÈLE. My God, it's true! And I adored you! I was yours, body and soul! I lived only for you! Now, it's all over.— But I still have some pride left! Don't imagine I'll stay here now, live with you, and take care of you! Never! I could never stand this! Now you may do what you like! Spend my dowry on your woman if you want! I won't be here — I'm going to my mother! Good-by! All this — this — Oh — help me — give me your arm — I — I can't —

[*She falls on the sofa in a faint.*]

ALBERT. Fainted! Adèle, Adèle! Poor little woman! — I *am* a beast! A brute! [*A pause.*] Well, what now? [*He rubs her hands, while speaking.*] The whole thing was absurd! I told Caroline not to detain me! Now what'll she do? Adèle will go to her mother; *she* at least will not refuse to see me! Will she, though? Of course? And Adèle loves me too well to leave me.— Well, there's no great harm. She had to find out, some day! It's happened this evening. I'm glad it's all over. We won't have any more trouble on that score, then. It's really much better this way. I like things perfectly open.— Whew, my hand is tired — she doesn't seem to be coming to.— I wonder what she'll say when she sees me? Cry, I suppose, and make a scene! — She's breathing regularly now. Good! — No more danger. I think I'll spare her my presence, and send the maid to look after her. Be so delicate! — I'll make it all up to her later. — Whew! I'm tired! [*Yawning.*] I'm going to bed.

[*He rings the bell, which is to the right of the fireplace, and goes out.*]

[CURTAIN.]

ACT III

[*Scene: The same as in the preceding acts. Mme. Viot, Marie, Adèle, and Albert are present.*]

ALBERT. Have a nice dinner, Mother-in-law?

MME. VIOT. We always have nice dinners at your house.

ALBERT. Good.— I'm in splendid spirits, aren't you?

MME. VIOT. I should think so!

ALBERT. This is indeed pleasant, now. [*To Adèle.*] Isn't it? And to think that three years ago, she wanted to leave me, go back to her mother! Do you remember, Adèle? And for what reason? Because I was not a model husband! Heavens, who *is* a model in this life? Not even you, in spite of your recent access of religion!

ADÈLE. If I lack something, it is because the good Lord isn't quite enough to insure my happiness!

ALBERT. Kiss me! How I love her! How I love her! My life would be empty without her. She is — she *is* an angel! Dear Adèle!

ADÈLE. It's all so strange. The evening I left here, after I fainted, I swore I would never put foot in the house again! I loathed, I hated you! But Mama talked and reasoned with me — then I came back. I'm not sorry for it — that is enough!

ALBERT. Charming!

MME. VIOT. You may well say it!

ALBERT. And I do.— And your dear sister, too. She doesn't say anything, but look at her: working —

MARIE. Yes.

ALBERT. Trousers for that youngster of yours?

MARIE. Yes. How fast he wears them out! How much he costs me, just for his trousers! The little rascal!

ALBERT. Why didn't you bring him this evening? We might have played soldiers!

MARIE. When he's with you, he's so naughty!

ALBERT. But very amusing! Wouldn't it be splendid to have a little fellow like that! [*To Adèle.*] Ah, Adèle — I don't blame you!

MARIE. Oh, well, let's hope —! If you're serious —!

ALBERT [*to Marie*]. You, you're a great one! — When does your husband return from Marseilles?

MARIE. To-morrow.

ALBERT. I'll tell him what you said. [*To Mme. Viot.*] Don't you agree with me? And you, dear Mother-in-law, you're simply wonderful! It's not my fault if I don't understand life as you do. I have the very devil of a disposition. Really, you do carry your — how many? — years: forty? Forty-five?

MME. VIOT. Flatterer!

ALBERT. But you like me to — to say these little things, to you, eh?

MME. VIOT. Yes — I'd rather hear agreeable than disagreeable things.

ALBERT. Ah! — Look, what's the dear lady knitting now? A comfortable for me?

MME. VIOT. For the poor.

ALBERT. The poor! She's always thinking of the poor! See here! I'm not going out this evening, I'm going to stay with my mother-in-law! No escapades to-day — bosom of the family and conjugal love!

MME. VIOT. Adorable boy!

ALBERT. But take care! One compliment too many and I'll take fright and go farther than you like! You laugh, but I'm serious.— When you're too free with me, I'm not responsible —

MME. VIOT. What a dear! [*Suddenly becoming pensive.*] That's the way he's always played on our feelings. You make us forget your bad actions so soon!

ALBERT. Who?

MME. VIOT. Tell me, you bad boy, how much is left of my daughter's dowry? Nothing! And yours? And the money you got from your parents? Not a sou! Between the two of you, you've squandered nearly a million francs! You have only your 15,000 francs' income to live on. And who gets a half of that? I don't dare mention the name! And I thought it was a great stroke of business to marry my daughter to you!

ALBERT. That's funny!

MME. VIOT. You certainly ran through that fortune fast enough.

ALBERT. Yes, fast enough! But then I'm a good fellow.

MME. VIOT. Yes, you are! — You're not in debt any longer, are you? You're not going to come to me again, as you did six months ago, and wheedle me into giving you my savings, for certain debts, gambling and others? Don't you ever win at your club?

ALBERT. Never!

ADÈLE. Let's not talk about that, Mother. It's so painful!

ALBERT [*laughing*]. Ah, your mother! Look at her face when she talks of money!

MME. VIOT. Oh, well, I — I must have money to live on. A great deal! You can never have too much. But I'm quite happy now; this morning I did a good stroke of business. I had a neat little pile of savings in my drawer; I took it to my broker, laid it all on his desk — twenty-five franc pieces, bills all tied together in little heaps of ten. He looked at me over the top of his spectacles — I took my time about it. After I'd counted it all — and it took a long time! — I said to him: "Put it all in good solid stocks. Good morning, M. Robillet!" He shook hands with me and bowed! — That's the sort of thing, I say, that's decidedly pleasant!

ALBERT. You are the queen of mothers-in-law, and Adèle is the queen of women! Work, my child! Respect the time-honored virtues: the thimble, the thread, and the needle — "Of those who worked for their daughters' trousseaux"— Who said that?

ADÈLE. Regnard, wasn't it?

MME. VIOT. No, no: Beranger!

ALBERT. Yes, of course.

MME. VIOT. What charming songs he's written, that Beranger! There's one my grandfather used to sing, I remember.

ALBERT. Whew! They used to sing Beranger to you?

MARIE. What was the song?

ALBERT. Sing it to us!

MME. VIOT. I don't remember it all.

ALBERT. The book is in my room, on the shelf. [*To Adèle.*] Get it for your mother. [*Adèle goes out.*] We'll sing it together: the matriarch singing in the midst of her children! The couplets of youth repeated in the accents of maturity. Ha! Ha! — [*He takes Mme. Viot in his arms.*] Now —! Can you remember?

[*Re-enter Adèle with the book and a letter.*]

ADÈLE [*to Albert*]. A note that was just brought for you.

ALBERT [*taking the letter*]. Thanks.

MME. VIOT. [*who has been reading*]. There, I knew it: "*Lisette's Infidelities.*"

ALBERT. Yes, I remember it.

MME. VIOT: [*singing, accompanied by Albert*].

"Oh, dear Lisette
Whose charms divine
Make my regret!
Oh, how I pine!
Thy cold disdain
I clearly see:
My sorrow's vain,
Thou'rt false to me!

ALBERT. [*singing loudly, as he opens the letter*].

> "Lisette, Lisette,
> Thou'rt false to me!
> Long life, grisette!
> Long life, Lisette,
> So drink to our love.

Oh, Heavens — [*He interrupts himself, terrified.*] Adèle, Mme. Viot! Mme. Chesneau! This is horrible! If you don't save me, I'm ruined!

ADÈLE. My God! What is it? Tell us!

MARIE. Tell us!

MME. VIOT. What is it?

ALBERT. If I don't have 200,000 francs by to-morrow morning, anything may happen to me!

MME. VIOT. Why?

ALBERT. Why? Why? This is why — well, it's not easy to say. Don't insist, please — please! I don't dare!

ADÈLE. Explain it; you must. What's the trouble?

MME. VIOT. We must know! —

ALBERT. It's a regular whirlwind — once you get started, there's no stopping! Horrible! — That damned Caroline! I told her no good would come of it! She hasn't the sense of a child!

MME. VIOT. Never mind that woman! Tell us, now.

ALBERT. Here then: since you so insist. I was terribly hard pressed for money, and at one time or another I took 200,000 francs of the company's funds.

ALL. Oh!

MME. VIOT. Lovely surprise!

ALBERT. If I don't refund the money to-morrow morning I'm ruined, dishonored, sent to jail! The directors have written that they are coming to inspect the office at eleven o'clock. They won't handle me with kid gloves, I can tell you! Swooping down on me like that! I'm not a regular thief, I suppose! I always meant to put it back, you know!

MME. VIOT. They all say that, but they never do it.

ALBERT. I couldn't, it wasn't my fault. I counted on another affair — which didn't materialize.

MME. VIOT. My death, of course!

ALBERT. No more than on anything else. I'm not to blame. You'll pay, won't you? I haven't a sou. Wait, yes: one hundred francs! Say something, for the love of Heaven!

MME. VIOT. You're a good-for-nothing! That's what I say!

ALBERT. Madame!

MME. VIOT. A good-for-nothing, I repeat! [*In an altered voice.*] But are you sure the directors are coming to-morrow?

ALBERT. Absolutely.

MME. VIOT. Fool!

ALBERT. Instead of insulting me, you might help me parry the blow. Now, Mme. Viot, answer me: I've got to get out of this. Loan me 200,000 francs! Only till to-morrow, till noon! Just let me have them in the safe when they come. I'll give them to you an hour after the directors leave. That's an idea! Come, say something — yes or no? I don't like you to be saying nothing at all!

ADÈLE. Let Mama have time to collect her thoughts, dear. Meantime, perhaps we can think of another way out of the difficulty.

ALBERT. You know very well there is no other.

ADÈLE. That's true: we have nothing. I see no way out — unless — yes, that will pay part of it — perhaps Mama will consent to pay the rest.

ALBERT. What do you mean?

ADÈLE. Why, if my dowry is all gone, I still have my laces — worth about 15,000 francs — then there are my jewels.

ALBERT. Good! Where are they?

ADÈLE. In the desk drawer.

ALBERT. I'll get them. [*He goes out.*]

MARIE. Poor child! This is awful! To have to sell your jewels, at your age! It's a pity!

ADÈLE. What else can we do? We have no time to lose. I'll sell them in the morning.

[*Albert re-enters.*]

[*To Albert*]. You have them?

ALBERT. All.

ADÈLE. Lay them on the table. Now give me a pencil and paper. Thanks. Lamp is low! [*She turns up the wick.*] There.— 200,000 francs, you say? Here's my diamond necklace. [*While she is speaking, Marie hands her the jewel boxes which she opens.*] What can I get for it? 25,000, let us say! How beautiful they are, this one especially! [*To Marie.*] Pretty, aren't they? Here's the bracelet: 4000. Now the cameo necklace — I've worn it only twice — 4,000. Ear-rings: 5,000. [*Taking them off.*] They stick a little — not used to coming off! [*Taking off her rings.*] Now the rings; the turquoises: 2,000.— I want to keep the ruby, it's my engagement ring!

MME. VIOT. Pleasant souvenir!

ALBERT. Sell it anyway!

ADÈLE. No, I don't want to sell it!

MME. VIOT. I'll buy back your earrings! For the sake of the family, I don't want you to part with them. Put them on again.

ADÈLE. Thank you! Thank you!

MME. VIOT. Don't thank me.

ADÈLE. That makes 55,000 francs I can furnish. That's all. Now, Mama?

MME. VIOT. Don't try to argue with me: I shan't pay a sou!

ADÈLE. You refuse?! It's impossible!

ALBERT. Now, Madame! —

MME. VIOT. Not a word from you, you miserable sneak!

ALBERT. Can't you listen to reason?

MME. VIOT. No impudence, please!

ALBERT. I'm no more impudent than you.

MME. VIOT. What's that?

ALBERT. No more impudent than you, I say!

MME. VIOT. You repeat it? I'm going home!

ALBERT. Sulky!

MME. VIOT. Sulky?! Sulky?!

ALBERT. Yes!

MME. VIOT. Take care, young man! I'll take hold of you —!

ALBERT. Scratch me, won't you?

MME. VIOT [*going toward Albert*]. Yes, I will! I'll —!

MARIE [*interfering*]. Mama! What a disgraceful scene! What if any one should come in! Really —!

ADÈLE. We're all very much upset — let's put an end to this. We must find 145,000 francs now.

MME. VIOT. I won't pay a sou! I won't see your grandfather's good money slip through this sieve! The poor old man would blush from Heaven if he saw me doing it!

ALBERT. Then, Madame, I shall be dishonored!

MME. VIOT. I won't pay, so there! If you were a real man, you would have blown your brains out twenty times by now instead of lowering yourself by asking me for the money!

ALBERT. My dear good lady, you're losing your senses.

MME. VIOT. Don't you call me your "dear good lady"! If I'm losing my senses, isn't it enough to make me with an idiot like you,—?

ALBERT. But think of the good name of the family!

MME. VIOT. The good name of the family has nothing to do with the case, Monsieur! Any one can tell you that! Every one knows my husband was a judge, that my grandfather was an advocate at Paris and my brother a notary. They will keep up our good name! The disgrace will be yours, and yours only!

ALBERT. Then you really refuse? Good! I know what to do now!

ADÈLE. Mama, he's going to kill himself!

ALBERT. No: I'm going to Brussels.

MME. VIOT. Am I not right, Marie?

MARIE. I think you had better pay, Mama — for the sake of your grandson —

ALBERT [*to Mme. Viot*]. You can afford it, you're rich! You admit having 600,000 francs, but you have a million!

MME. VIOT [*furiously*]. I'm not rich! — And what if I were? I couldn't keep my money long, Heaven knows! "You're rich!" Lovely! Haven't I plenty of ways to spend my money? That fool carriage, which I never use — that you force me to keep for the sake of appearances! Only this morning do you know what I paid my architect? A hundred and fifteen francs just for fixing the roof!

ADÈLE. But that's not what we're discussing, Mama!

MME. VIOT. And the taxes! What taxes the Government makes me pay! They're a pack of thieves! This is a fine Republic that Monsieur there helps support! Ha! — Meantime, I pay! The big fortunes of twenty years ago are hardly enough to run a poor man's family now. And you talk of getting more money out of me! It's ridiculous. Everybody's against me! Not one of you takes my side! At my age there's only one thing for me to do: live in the desert or the work-house! That's a fine idea now. Then you'd be rid of me. I could get along on a thousand francs a year, and then you could squander my fortune to your heart's content!

MARIE. Well, if you ask my advice, I'll tell you what I think.

MME. VIOT. Thank you, dear children. I'll tell you one thing, though: in my father's house, no one would have dared raise his voice against mother,— the way you're doing this moment. You should have heard your poor uncle trying to discuss and advise.

MARIE. Wouldn't they let him even when they asked for his advice?

MME. VIOT. Not even then! My father would have sent him to his room, and told him to mind his own business. But times have changed, no one respects his parents nowadays —!

ADÈLE. But we respect you, Mama!

MME. VIOT [*furiously*]. You don't! You don't respect me! I'm going home, sell my furniture, lock the door, and leave — to-morrow morning —

ALBERT. For the work-house!

MME. VIOT. No, for my house in the country, at Romilly. I'm going to spend the rest of my life in the woods — with the animals — that treat me better than human beings! There at least I won't be troubled with children who take all my money — sons-in-law that insult and disgrace me!

ALBERT. Good! Then don't pay! It was only for your sake I said anything about this matter. Now I know what to do. I'm going to live in Brussels, where I have good friends. I'll begin all over again. I won't listen to any more of your rigmaroles! Not a bit of it. I exposed the whole situation to you: frankly, honestly, amicably. Now I wash my hands of it. Only, I must confess that I am greatly surprised. I had thought that a good sensible woman like you would have preferred to make a small temporary sacrifice to having a son-in-law in Belgium! You could have had your money back any time you cared to ask for it. It would be in the bank, as safe as could be. But I shan't say anything more: if you're tired of my sermonizing, so am I. Better come to some decision among yourselves. I give you an hour!

[*He pours out a glass of water for himself.*]

MME. VIOT. You *are* giving us a sermon now!

ALBERT. Do you want me to go?

ADÈLE. No, stay. Don't listen to him, Mama! Really, you're not very generous!

MME. VIOT. What? Aren't you satisfied with his having squandered your whole dowry? Do you want him to squander your inheritance?

ADÈLE. His interests just now are greater than mine. You say that we don't keep together very well as a family. You've told me twenty times that the members of a family ought to help one another in times of danger. You ought to practise what you preach! Think of the dishonor this affair would be to all of us. Think of your grandson too; you have no right to compromise *his* future. He will marry some day, he will try to marry into an honorable family. He'll not be able to: people won't allow their daughters to form alliances with such as we are.— You must pay, you see. Our honor, our peace of mind, forces you to do it, not to speak of our reputation and even our common material interests. If I can't persuade you, then just think it all over to yourself. What would father have done?

MME. VIOT. Your father?

ADÈLE. Father would have payed.

MME. VIOT [*after a pause*]. Do what you like, only I warn you, you shan't touch my stocks in the Eastern Railway.

ALBERT. But those are the easiest to dispose of at once.

MME. VIOT. You shan't touch them!

ADÈLE. Then where can we get the money?

MME. VIOT. Ask Marie, she knows about my business affairs.

MARIE. I know nothing whatsoever.— My time is spent only in being with you and loving you, Mama!

ADÈLE. How are we to go about raising the money? Do you get immediate cash on notes?

MME. VIOT. Ask your husband! He knows about notes!

ADÈLE. Very well.— You said the other day that you had 100,000 francs' worth of Eastern Railway stocks at your broker's.

MARIE. A hundred and seven thousand five hundred.

MME. VIOT. I think I said something about not touching those stocks!

ADÈLE. Well, we —

MME. VIOT. Try the *Andalusian Railway,* not the others.

ADÈLE. Are they good? I don't know. Albert, you ought to?

ALBERT. No, they don't move. Can't sell them!

MME. VIOT. How's that? They went down lately — they certainly *do* move!

ALBERT. We're joking!

MME. VIOT. Well, then, sell the Eastern Stocks, if you insist! Only you're robbing me; I will say that.

ADÈLE [*writing*]. 107,500 plus 55,000. That makes —

MME. VIOT. Ha!

ADÈLE [*hesitating*]. 160——

MME. VIOT. 162,500!

ADÈLE. There are still 42,500 francs needed. We'll get that from your other holdings: *Orleans Railway, Paris-Lyons, Mediterranean,* etc.

MME. VIOT. What about the *Andalusian Railway?*

ADÈLE [*without listening*]. That makes 205,-000 francs.— Five thousand too much!

MME. VIOT [*satirically*]. And some more while you are about it!

ADÈLE. What's the matter?

MME. VIOT. Your addition is wrong.

ALBERT [*embarrassed*]. No, it's right. I took 205,000 francs from the office — I said 200,-000 before, because it was a convenient sum.

ADÈLE. See, Mother?

MME. VIOT. I do see. But I refuse to give the extra 5000 francs!

ADÈLE. What are 5000 francs when you're already paying 145,000?

MME. VIOT [*calmly*]. I refuse!

ADÈLE. For the sake of your grandchild!

MME. VIOT. I refuse!

MARIE. The stocks are in your desk in the little parlor!

MME. VIOT [*throwing her keys on the floor*]. There! Take my keys. You're robbers! Now, whoever of you two dares pick up the keys, I swear before the Lord I will disinherit! —

[*Marie, who has stooped to pick up the keys, quickly rises.*]

ADÈLE [*picking them up.— To Albert*]. Come!

[*Adèle and Albert go out.*]

MARIE [*after a pause*]. Let's at least follow them. We don't want them to turn everything upside down!

MME. VIOT. Of course not.

MARIE. When we're alone, we must have a little talk.

MME. VIOT. About what?

MARIE. The future. A thing like this might happen more than once with a son-in-law like Albert. He'd ruin us all!

MME. VIOT. But what can we do about it?

MARIE. Of course, I advise against divorce — it would be against the Church, but a separation —!

MME. VIOT. No, no, no. Once lose hold of Albert, and I'd never see my money again!

MARIE. Would you prefer to have him run through another 200,000?

MME. VIOT. Besides, you can't get a separation for that reason.

MARIE. We're quite within our rights. Two

or three times Albert has brought this mistress here — this summer — I know it! — While you and Adèle were at Romilly!

MME. VIOT. But what will people say?

MARIE. That you are making the best of a bad job. It was an unwise marriage. I advised you against it, God knows!

[*They go out, left.*]

[CURTAIN.]

ACT IV

[*The same scene as in the preceding acts. Adèle is present. Marie enters a moment later.*]

MARIE. How are you?

ADÈLE. Well, thanks, dear. Sit down.

MARIE. I'm not in the way?

ADÈLE. No, no. Albert is still at the office. I felt a little lonely, all by myself.

MARIE. I wanted to say something about Albert. How is he behaving?

ADÈLE. He's lovely, very kind and considerate just now. He seems very much cut up over what's happened. I feel that he bitterly repents it, and is doing everything he can to make amends for that affair of nearly a year ago.

MARIE. Yes.—

ADÈLE. The other evening he took me to the theater — that's an indication. He doesn't do it often, Heaven knews! That's a sure sign of his repentance.

MARIE. How about the money he owes Mama? Does he think about that — ever?

ADÈLE. I'm always talking to him about it. I have to be very careful, for he doesn't like to be reminded. But business is business — this year hasn't been a very good one for us: stocks haven't been paying dividends. So you understand —

MARIE. Yes, it is bothersome. Of course if we were only sure of the future, everything would be all right. Unfortunately, we're not. Who knows? A character of his sort — not sure of himself, you know — then that woman, who seems to have a greater hold on him than ever. And that money-box, always within his reach, to which he alone has the key! I'm afraid to think of it!

ADÈLE. Let's not say anything about it, please!

MARIE. But we must!

ADÈLE. Why? We can do nothing.

MARIE. We can discuss the matter.

ADÈLE. Discuss?

MARIE. Yes.

ADÈLE. What do you mean by that?

MARIE. I mean — that Mama thinks so too. I'm only speaking for her, you understand? If I were the only one concerned, why then —! Such matters don't interest me personally in the least!

ADÈLE. Dear sister!

MARIE. How I've had to take your part against Mama! Do you know, she blames you now for everything — just as if it were your fault, dear!

ADÈLE. Poor Mama! She'll never forgive me for all this trouble. But it's really not been my fault.

MARIE. I said we might discuss ways and means in order to guard against another catastrophe in the future. The best plan would be a simple separation from your husband.

ADÈLE. You want me to apply for a separation? What would Albert do without me?

MARIE. Think, my dear, think. It's for your good. Really, you're not in love with your husband. What if he should play some new pranks — think what would happen? We've all suffered, you especially, from his reckless extravagance — and poor Mama! She's broken-hearted to see all her savings go like this. It's taken her nearly a year to recover from that last shock. She's aged ten years! She had such a splendid appetite, and now she hardly eats anything at all. She's merely the wreck of her former self. [*Overcome with emotion.*] What — what if we should lose her?!

ADÈLE. But Mama is very well.

MARIE. There you're mistaken.

ADÈLE. Not at all!

MARIE. My heart tells me I know the truth. You, for instance, what state do you imagine you are in now?

ADÈLE. I'm very well.

MARIE. Very well? My dear sister, don't deceive yourself: you've changed vastly. Mama and I have spent many a sleepless night worrying about you — your hollow cheeks, sunk eyes, those awful headaches of yours! You look like a little martyr! You might easily succumb to new shocks — the life your husband is leading might — what if we should lose you? If God were to take you from us! I'm sick at the very thought! No, no, not that! to lose you, little sister! I can't even think of it! — Make it a legal separation, do!

ADÈLE. Don't be alarmed, dear, I'm perfectly well.

MARIE. A sister's heart cannot be mistaken!

ADÈLE. But it is, for I'm in perfect health.

MARIE. Really?

ADÈLE. Yes!

MARIE. Then —

ADÈLE. Let's not say anything more about it —

MARIE. You certainly are to be pitied. I understand your troubles and worries. This everlasting wrangling is a terrible thing in a family like ours. The situation is very critical. Now, you're a reasonable person; I ask you, have you the right to drag your mother and sister into all this? Sacrifice us?

ADÈLE. What — you?

MARIE [*sweetly*]. Yes, me! You really must have some consideration for others. I at least have some rights. And our dear mother — whom God spare to us a long while yet! — cannot live forever! I can't allow Albert to go on squandering money as he does, and endanger my own future. On Mama's death I am to get 300,000 francs. Up to now, your share only has been touched — but a man like your husband wouldn't stop short of taking the whole fortune. Your nephew too must not be forgotten. He mustn't be deprived of his share. No, Mama is no longer young, and I must think of these things. We must keep a careful guard on the money that remains — the money that will one day be ours — and see that Mama doesn't use it up. What do you say? Tell me.

ADÈLE [*energetically, after a pause*]. No, I shall not ask for a separation!

MARIE. You're wrong, child.

ADÈLE. But you're considering only the financial side of the question.

MARIE. What other side is there — in your relations with Albert?

ADÈLE. A great deal that you don't seem to take into account. First there is love, the basis of family life.

MARIE. Money is the basis of family life.

ADÈLE. I don't agree with you.— Then there's my duty as a Christian wife: I should stand by my husband and obey him —

MARIE. How about your mother?

ADÈLE. Not now! Anyway, I want Albert!

MARIE. A man of his sort!

ADÈLE [*nettled*]. Yes, a man of his sort! I advise you not to say anything against him. He's very intelligent, and he's a hard and faithful worker. That engine he invented — it was all in the papers — not every one can do that!

MARIE [*also nettled*]. Do you say that for my husband's benefit?

ADÈLE. For him — and everybody, my dear.

MARIE. Gustave's name has not appeared in the newspapers, but he might have it if he liked!

ADÈLE. What did he invent?

MARIE. You persist in attacking him?

ADÈLE. You attacked Albert; I don't see why I shouldn't do the same to Gustave?

MARIE. But —

ADÈLE [*tenderly*]. Let's drop it, please. Albert is good to me, tender and loving. Sometimes he caresses me, and says my hair is prettier than hers — the other's. And I'm so grateful! I think him charming, and he's my husband.

MARIE. What difference does that make?

ADÈLE. I love him! If you want to know the whole truth: I've struggled hard — I may be weak — but I am in the right, I believe — I belong to him body and soul, in spite of his infidelity — I simply can't do without him.

MARIE [*disgusted*]. Oh!

ADÈLE. It's all very well for you to talk, with a husband like yours!

MARIE. If Gustave ever deceived me, all would be over between us!

ADÈLE. Well, I forgave my husband. I once thought of leaving him, when I first learned the truth,— put an end to everything in true dramatic style. I tried to go away, but you and Mama persuaded me to return to him. Even then I struggled against my inclinations, I hardly spoke a word to him,— avoided him. I even went to my confessor about it. My youth, my enthusiasm — all — in time I again became his wife, and I was only too happy to find that he still had some affection for me!

MARIE. But think of your situation now! To think that Albert brazenly speaks to you about his mistress, in your ordinary conversation! Consider what your love will lead you to! You're only a tool in his hands — you're bound hand and foot. See what your weakness has already cost you! How much more may it cost! Now if you would only consent to a separation —

ADÈLE. No, no, no, I'll not consent. That

would be too terrible. I feel positive of that. I am a little ashamed, and I do suffer; perhaps I'm condemning myself to a life of torture, to ruin and misery — but I don't care. Call it passion, worse than passion; Albert is necessary to my life. You may tell that to Mama, to your husband, to everybody. Your "financial" questions don't interest me. And then, you ought to leave me with my husband, for you gave him to me!

MARIE [*after a pause*]. Very well! I'm not the only one concerned. I am authorized to say that if you don't consent to an immediate separation, Mama will have nothing further to do with you.

ADÈLE. Mama?

MARIE. Yes — she is very angry with you. Now what do you say?

ADÈLE. So much the worse!

MARIE. Good. Only I advise you to persuade your husband to pay his debt. Pressure may be brought to bear on him.

ADÈLE. You are right. It will be very hard, but I'll do my best. I'll sacrifice, if need be.

MARIE. You know my feelings toward you, dearest. Don't consider me: I've done my best to smooth things over. You don't blame me, do you? I'd be so sorry!

ADÈLE. No, my dear sister, I know your love for me!

MARIE. Kiss me.

ADÈLE [*kissing her*]. With all my heart!

MARIE. And now, good-by. Speak to your husband.

ADÈLE. As soon as he comes.

[*Marie goes out.*]

ADÈLE. Mama have nothing more to do with me? How queer that sounds! When I was a little girl and heard about children falling out with their parents, it seemed ridiculous — especially on the part of the children. Now here *I* am! And am I really to blame? Not to see Mama any more! I remember when she took me to school, and scolded me in the street: "Walk quickly now, or we'll be late!" If I could only make Albert pay! He could if he wanted to. I'll speak to him to-night. I hope I'm successful this time! There he is — courage!

[*Enter Albert.*]

ADÈLE. Good evening, dear!

ALBERT. Good evening.

ADÈLE. I'm so glad to see you!

ALBERT. Is dinner nearly ready?

ADÈLE. It isn't time yet. No — only half past six.

ALBERT. I'm very busy: I must go out.

ADÈLE. I'll have dinner hurried.

ALBERT. Please.

ADÈLE. You'll like the dinner — too bad you haven't much time. There's some lovely lamb, with potatoes — and — what do you think? Soufflé with apricots! You like that, don't you?

ALBERT. Yes, yes.

ADÈLE. See how I think of you! But that's not all. I made a great find at the *Bon Marché*. Guess?

ALBERT. I'm no good at guessing.

ADÈLE. Ties: the kind you like — satin, that you tie yourself.

ALBERT. Like Colin's?

ADÈLE. Isn't that the kind you like?

ALBERT. Oh, yes, they're as good as any other.

ADÈLE. They're beautiful shades: two blue ones with white spots, two black ones with blue figures. You can wear one for this evening. Would you like to see them?

ALBERT. I don't care. Leave them in my room.

ADÈLE. I got you some gloves too — you'll like them —

ALBERT. Yes, yes, good!

ADÈLE. Nice of me, wasn't it? You can't say I don't take good care of you, can you? — Why don't you kiss your wife?

ALBERT. There! [*He kisses her perfunctorily. A pause.*]

ADÈLE. Business picking up? Are you more hopeful?

ALBERT [*reading a newspaper*]. About the same.

ADÈLE. No rise?

ALBERT. No rise, no rise. You can't tell. Business is business, it changes from day to day. I don't like to discuss these matters with women: they understand nothing about it all. Let me read my paper. I'm out of humor! [*A pause.*]

ADÈLE. I know it's not pleasant, but while we're on the subject, you must remember that we owe Mama money: 150,000 francs, of which we haven't paid back one sou.

ALBERT. I advise you to ask for money now! Caroline asked for some this morning — Ha!

ADÈLE. It isn't for myself! Mama has the

right to ask for her money. [*Very quietly.*] That money was a loan, not a gift!

ALBERT. Your mother is an old miser — I'll not trouble with her!

ADÈLE. Mama wants to keep the family fortune intact. She's very conservative about it; she belongs to the old school. She would never get over it if the fortune at her death were less than what it was when she inherited it. It's only to her credit that she feels as she does.

ALBERT. I tell you she's an old miser!

ADÈLE. That doesn't make us any less her debtors. You can't imagine how worried I am over this. You know how I economize! My household expenses are very small, I wear dresses for three years, our table is quite modest — two courses at each meal —. And yet I can't save up enough to pay back more than a fraction. If you could only let me have a little more money. You spend a great deal yourself — I'm not blaming you — that's your affair,— only if you could economize a little? If I could just give back a thousand francs! It would be a load off my shoulders! Think if she'd have nothing more to do with us —

ALBERT. I'll pay everything back in due time. Meanwhile she may do what she likes. Do you want me to kill myself with work in order to flatter a millionaire?

ADÈLE. My dear good sister —

ALBERT. "Good" sister! Another of your notions!

ADÈLE. However that may be, Marie told me just now that Mama was very angry with us.

ALBERT. She can't disinherit you, can she?

There's the law, that's all that's necessary. I have a regular contract, thank God!

ADÈLE. You might try to be on good terms with her!

ALBERT. To be grateful? Rot!

ADÈLE. No, but I love Mama, and I want to avoid a rupture.

ALBERT. Ha! Ha!

ADÈLE [*insisting*]. Yet — we owe her 150,-000 francs. Think of it — if we could only —

ALBERT [*getting angry*]. That's enough! And your mother can go hang! She's been stingy enough lately. When I used to be in need of money, I managed to extract fifteen louis from her — when she was in the mood —. There was nothing wrong in that: I merely followed the example of your "good" sister. *She* knows how to exploit the old lady. She knows every movement — she keeps mighty close watch! How do you know but that she'll take the 150,000 francs that are still due us? By God, if I felt sure of that I'd wring your sister's neck, that dear sister who bears, as she says, the same name as the Holy Virgin! Little good it does me if I ask for money occasionally. Of course, *you* don't care, you're always up in the clouds! It doesn't affect you! *I* have responsibilities and worries, I have two households to support! With you and Caroline —! The pair of you! — If I only had your dowry now —! Ha! It's taken flight — not much, for that matter — a little two-by-four dowry that kept us hardly two years! And now here your mother comes asking for her cursed money! Why doesn't she ask me to support her, your sister, your brother-in-law, your nephew — the whole crew?! I see they're trying to make a fool of me. That's what they're doing! Let's cut it short now: I won't be the stalking horse for the family —!

ADÈLE. How *can* you say that, dear?

ALBERT. I repeat it: the stalking-horse of the whole family! And I thought I was doing a good stroke of business! Such — such indelicacy! And she spends all her time casting that damned 150,000 francs in my teeth. A pretty state of affairs! And how I get blamed, whew! Simply because they did me a favor any one would do! As a rule when any one obliges a friend, he has the common decency not to make the obligation felt. The lender tries to make the borrower forget. It should be a pleasure to do a fellow-being a service — the offer should be repeated! It's one of the joys of life, and I pity the people who can't see it in that light. But *this* business, oh, my! And with me, who have been brought up where people have some delicacy of sentiment — Ha!

ADÈLE. You have no reason to complain.

ALBERT. Of course I have. How can I live with people who don't understand me? I'm paying back that money merely by remaining among you. And a fine family you are! Sitting around all day knitting socks — with no culture, no knowledge of the world. A mother who is a miser, a sister not very different from her — a brother-in-law —! Savages! — And do you imagine that you are anything remarkable? Pretty? You've lived so long with your mother that you've begun to look like her. I sometimes mistake you for her! Intelligent, spirituelle? You do nothing but make trouble in the family, and get me disliked! You join them to make my life miserable! If you want to know the truth, you're a little fool, with your love and your whimpering and your prayers and your priests and your God! Good Lord! — And — Then our having no children —! You —! [1]

ADÈLE. Albert!

ALBERT. Now about your mother —!

ADÈLE [*crying, but with energy*]. No, no, stop it! You have no right to say such terrible things about people who never did you wrong! I know you don't love *me* — but I won't allow you to say those things about my family — Never!

ALBERT [*furiously*]. And I tell you your mother is an old scarecrow, do you hear?

ADÈLE [*choking*]. I advise you not to say anything more about my mother before me —! Nor before any one else! You are the last one who has a right to! You know what might be said of you —!

ALBERT [*enraged*]. What?

ADÈLE. You know very well.

ALBERT. Say it!

ADÈLE. I wouldn't take the trouble! I wouldn't!

ALBERT. Go on — I'd just like to hear.

ADÈLE. Very well, then — you have — stolen — There!

[1] The exact lines ("Ton bon Dieu! . . . Couche donc avec, puisque tu l'aimes tant! Il te fera peut-être un enfant, lui! Dire que tu n'as pas même été capable de faire un enfant!") are of a brutality so revolting that I have substituted a milder line, containing something of the spirit of the original.— TR.

ALBERT [*menacingly*]. I'm a thief? I'm a thief? Now I'll show you how I appreciate the information!

ADÈLE [*terrified*]. What — what are you going to do?

ALBERT. I'm a thief, am I ?

[*He seizes her by the shoulders.*]

ADÈLE. Albert — Albert — Don't!

ALBERT. If you want to know: I detest you, hate you! Get out, now! I've seen enough of you! You damned —!

ADÈLE. Let go! Let go! You're hurting me! You have no right to treat me like this! Oh! — Help! I'm —!

ALBERT [*throwing her to the floor*]. There!

ADÈLE [*in agony*]. Oh! [*Albert sits down. Adèle slowly rises.*]

ALBERT [*as if about to throw her down again*]. Get out.

[*Adèle goes out at the back.*]

ALBERT [*calmly lighting a cigarette*]. Feel relieved! [*Dreamily*]. I suppose she'll ask for a separation now!

[CURTAIN.]

ACT V

[*The same scene as in the preceding acts. Adèle, Mme. Viot, and Marie are present.*]

MME. VIOT. And how are you this evening, dear?

ADÈLE. Still a bit sick — it's my stomach.

MME. VIOT. Come, now, it's nothing serious. You imagine much worse than it is. How you worry! At my age I don't like to hear about sickness, you know. Don't pull that long face — be gay. We've come up to talk over a serious matter.

ADÈLE. All right, Mama.

MARIE. Poor child!

MME. VIOT. What are you working at?

ADÈLE. I'm knitting a vest for the poor.

MME. VIOT. Lay it aside and listen to us. Marie, will you begin?

MARIE. No, Mama, I'd rather you did. In questions of money I'm so stupid.

ADÈLE. It's about money? Still?

MME. VIOT. Yes. For six months you've been separated from your husband — your eyes were opened at last. You've been living practically with us, but now you must establish yourself permanently, so that the rights of all of us shall not suffer. At first I had thought of taking you with us, but our habits, our manner of living, are so different! You are, you must admit, a little hard to get along with — you are wilful, headstrong — we couldn't get on well, I fear. Then if I took you it would be as much as a confession of defeat before the world, and I don't want people to imagine that anything's wrong — for the sake of the good name of the family. In case they do suspect, I don't want to have it said that I was to blame. Here's what we've decided, your sister and I: we want you to live here, by yourself, comfortably and respectably.

MARIE. Each of us in his own home — that's the best way.

MME. VIOT. It's easy to see that you can't count on that 2,000 francs' alimony your husband should pay you. I know very well he can't afford the money. We've therefore arranged to allow you an income of 5,000 francs a year. The capital will be yours: about 150,000 francs — your share of the family fortune. That's the easiest way: then I shan't be bothered with continual requests for assistance. You may have your breakfasts with me. Isn't that fair?

ADÈLE. Yes, Mama, I see —

MME. VIOT. You don't seem very satisfied. We've made out a complete budget for you. Listen: 5,000 francs a year is 416 francs 30 centimes a month. That's a good round sum! Household expenses for yourself and two servants —

ADÈLE. I'll not need the butler.

MME. VIOT. And stay alone with the maid? Never! You must think of appearances! This money is not for amusements, you understand —

not to allow you to knit vests for the poor — you must live so that no one can point a finger at us. To continue: household expenses for you and two servants: 150 francs. That's plenty. Wages: 130 francs. That leaves 136 — say 130. Clothes: nothing — nothing, too, for the upkeep of the house. As you make your own dresses, and take good care not to burn too much gas — you'll have more than enough. For that matter, you'll be richer than I! But you can't do as you did at my place at lunch to-day — order a boiled egg when there were plenty of fried potatoes. An egg is an egg.

ADÈLE. I wasn't feeling well this morning —

MME. VIOT. We'll let that pass. Now for your present lease: I'll leave that to you. I hope you will allow me to pay as little as possible. You see, you're really living on us. Don't forget that!

ADÈLE. No, Mama, I shan't. Only, while we're on the subject, there's one thing I should like to say. If I keep this apartment, 5,000 francs will be nothing at all — if I continue to live in the same style as before. With all your money, couldn't you afford —?

MME. VIOT. No, certainly not — if you begin to beg again —

ADÈLE. Consider that I've said nothing, if you get angry with me!

MME. VIOT. Well, I am. You're always that way: you're never satisfied. Haven't I done enough for you? If your children cost you as much as mine, I advise you to have very few! That is, if you'd like to have a bite to eat in your old age!

ADÈLE [*sobbing.*] Mama, Mama, are you blaming me for all that's happened? I can't say a thing now, it seems, without your flying into a rage! It's dreadful.

MME. VIOT. It's more dreadful to be drained of your money, the way I've been!

ADÈLE. Is that my fault?

MME. VIOT. Perhaps it's mine? I advise you to complain! I've had a fine time between you and that husband of yours! A fine specimen you brought into the family!

ADÈLE. Who picked him out for me?

MME. VIOT. You should have resisted, or else managed to get along with him better, instead of always taking his part against me! You've admired him so much that you begin to look like him! When I look at you, I tell you, I think it's he himself —!

ADÈLE. But —

MME. VIOT. Of course, in one way he's a nice fellow — I can't deny that. He always behaved very decently to me. Only, like all men, he had to be led with a string. You spoiled him, you let him go — through your own weakness. You thought him wonderful, distinguished! When I think of a daughter of mine being so — so much the slave of her passions — Oh! Like a common woman of the streets! That's the ruination of families! You think it's all very well — you didn't have to pay the piper! You just put your hand in other people's pockets —!

ADÈLE. Mama!

MARIE [*apparently much moved*]. Now, now! —

MME. VIOT. To think of all I was going to do with my money — I had a splendid opportunity — some stocks your poor father bought dirt-cheap just after the Revolution of '48. I had a lot of *Bank of France* stocks — I'd saved up for twenty years to buy them. Everybody said I was very lucky to get them. My friend, Mme. Renaudy, would have given anything to have them! Then the *Andalusian Railway* — no, those you let me keep! Thanks! Then the *Paris-Lyons, Mediterranean,* and the *Orleans Railway!* And the *Eastern!* Thanks to you, the fortune laid up by generation after generation of honest men, and which I was proud to guard, has now dwindled so that I am actually ashamed — it's never happened before in our family — and now! — while I was administering it — !

ADÈLE [*sobbing*]. I — I wish I had died long ago, and spared you all this trouble you're now blaming me for!

MME. VIOT [*furiously*]. Good Heavens, there are times when I wonder whether it wouldn't have been better!

ADÈLE [*sadly*]. Oh!

MARIE. Mama! Think of what you're saying! Poor Adèle!

[*A long pause.*]

MME. VIOT. Now, for all these reasons you are to have 5,000 francs' income, and not another sou — you ought to be thankful for that! I ask only one thing: that you will leave the capital — 150,000 francs — to Marie. You understand? To no one else! I don't want that money to go out of the family. Enough has gone already.

MARIE. I don't want to take advantage of your generosity, dear. I ask only one thing of Heaven: to take me before it does you. I couldn't survive you! I couldn't!

MME. VIOT. Then, you agree?

ADÈLE. Yes, Mama.

MME. VIOT. No dividing the capital! No remembrances or presents?

ADÈLE. No, Mama.

MME. VIOT. It's nine o'clock, I'm going home — I have to figure up my accounts. Oh, here are 300 francs, you may pay me back out of your allowance. [*Pointing to the notes she has given Adèle.*] Count them — I might be cheating you! — To-morrow we'll begin our new life: come to lunch. You may have boiled eggs. Good-night. Don't be extravagant, now!

MARIE [*to Adèle*]. Good-night, dear. I'm going home: my husband's waiting for me.

[*Mme. Viot and Marie kiss Adèle, and go out.*]

ADÈLE. Five thousand francs! How can I ever live on it? And they told me when I was married I should have a hundred thousand a year some day! Five thousand! Well, I must do my best! [*A pause.*] And he? What is he doing? What will become of him? Marie says her husband is waiting for her — I must stay here alone! — If I only heard something of *him!* — But if I must become used to the thought of doing without him, I must. I shall, in time. I've been pretty philosophical about it all lately. My life from now on will be lonely, I see that, but quiet and peaceful. I can at least take care of the little money I have.— That's something. What *is* the matter with me to-night? I'm a coward! — Where can he be? What is he doing?

[*Enter Albert, looking aged and ill-kempt.*]

ADÈLE. You?!

ALBERT. Yes, I. Don't call! You have nothing to be afraid of —

ADÈLE. If Mama knew —!

ALBERT. She's safe at home by now. I'll not stay long.

ADÈLE. Why have you come?

ALBERT. First to find out how you were: — you're not well, are you?

ADÈLE. No — but you can't stay here!

ALBERT. Stop, I have something important to say to you. I see my presence is disagreeable to you — so I'll stay only a moment.— You must have forgiven me by now? You know I was all out of humor that day! I'm not usually like that! You don't blame me, do you? Do you?

ADÈLE [*after a pause*]. How do I know?

ALBERT. See — you don't really blame me.— [*A pause.*]

ADÈLE [*looking at him*]. What *is* the matter?

ALBERT. Things haven't gone well. I've had no luck. I'm not like every one.

ADÈLE. What do you mean?

ALBERT. Ah, that's so: you're not to be envied, yourself!

ADÈLE. Now, what have you come for?

ALBERT. Well — may I sit down?

ADÈLE. Yes.

ALBERT. After the separation I went on with my work at the office. Then — well, I was unfortunate — the cash-box — Oh, nothing much this time: 10,000 francs! I was found out and shown the door. They were decent enough to me — they didn't let it get about. Only I was out of a job. Then I lived from hand to mouth — translated, addressed envelopes for circulars. See that pamphlet on the table? I wrote the address. Didn't you recognize my writing? — Then I — I've come to ask you to loan me a little — until I get on my feet again. Only till then! Your mother must give you an allowance? It would be a great help to me. If I don't have 300 francs to-night, God only knows what'll happen to me!

ADÈLE. Three hundred francs! That's a whole month's allowance. I don't keep things on the scale we used to!

ALBERT. Is that all you have?

ADÈLE. Not a sou more! Mama gave me a capital of 150,000 francs! Figure it up!

ALBERT. Then you can't let me have anything?

ADÈLE. If I did, how could I live?

ALBERT. There's your mother! [*A pause.*]

ADÈLE. Tell me the truth: are those 300 francs for yourself?

ALBERT [*vivaciously*]. Yes, yes. Don't imagine they're for her! I promise, I never see her!

ADÈLE. There's no need defending yourself so hotly! If it's true, why I —

ALBERT. Well —

ADÈLE. Be frank, I'd rather you were.

ALBERT [*after a pause*]. Well, yes, it is for her!

ADÈLE. Ah!

ALBERT. Jealous? What difference can that make to you now? We're separated. But you needn't think I'm happy. What scenes, what wailing — pitched battles! [*Sobbing.*] This morning she left me! Stay with me, Adèle! Don't send me away! *You* are good! It's a great relief to confide in you! — Yes, she left me. I went there this morning at eleven, as I usually do, for lunch. I kissed her, and then she asked me the first thing whether I had the 300 francs I'd promised. I told her I hadn't. Then, without a word, she said: "Get out, you old fool!" — She, she who told me I was the dearest being to her in the world! My God, Adèle! I don't know what to do! —

ADÈLE [*after a pause*]. There, there, don't go on like that! Here's your money, take it!

ALBERT. You're an angel! *You* understand me!

ADÈLE. Yes, I do understand you — better than you imagine. You love that woman the way I have loved you!

ALBERT. Thank you, thank you. You *are* good! If you knew what it cost me to ask you for money! I was afraid of your mother.— Now let's talk about something else.— How are you? Stomach still trouble you? You don't look very sick. Do you take good care of yourself?

ADÈLE. Yes — only you had better go now. If Mama were to know I had received you, and given you money, she would never forgive me.

ALBERT. One minute more! It's so comfortable here. You don't seem to realize it, but

I'm mighty glad to see you again! And are you glad —?

ADÈLE [*with deep feeling*]. I am!

ALBERT [*gaily*]. Tell me, your mother —?

ADÈLE. Yes, my mother?

ALBERT. She's not nice to you, eh?

ADÈLE. She must lay the blame on some one for all the money she's lost. She blames me for having married you — she says I was too easily influenced by you. She was right, too. You knew how to get anything you liked from me — I'd have let you get every sou I had. But I believe all women who loved as I did are like me. My mother is wrong in putting all the blame on me. I have suffered —!

ALBERT. But with all her money — and she has more than you think — she's allowed you only 5,000 francs? The old —!

ADÈLE [*smiling*]. Not a sou more.

ALBERT. You might occasionally get a little more.

ADÈLE. Yes, but what a time I'd have! Mama is positively ferocious.

ALBERT. I'm really surprised she doesn't ask you to cut down expenses!

ADÈLE. She does!

ALBERT. No?

ADÈLE. Yes, she does.

ALBERT. Well, I never! Such stinginess!

ADÈLE. They are a little careful! It's simply their nature.

ALBERT. Not much like me!

ADÈLE [*smiling genially*]. I should think not!

ALBERT. Makes you laugh, doesn't it?

ADÈLE. It all seems so long ago.

ALBERT. Poor dear! Always so patient and sweet! — And *I*, I'm not really so terrible, after all. Luck's been against me, that's all. You know I loved you — infinitely more than I did the other. My pleasantest hours have been passed with you. But, then, you can't fight against your destiny, that has been my misfortune. Dear Adèle.

ADÈLE [*troubled*]. Don't let's think of the past. We must be reasonable — you must go now —

ALBERT. So soon?

ADÈLE. Yes, you must. No good will come of our staying together.

ALBERT. I'll go, then, but not before I've kissed you and thanked you. I owe you at least that! Will you let me?

ADÈLE [*allowing him to kiss her*]. If you like.

ALBERT. On the neck — as I used to, when I was in a good humor — remember? [*He kisses her.*] Nice, eh?

ADÈLE [*overcome*]. Stop, stop, Albert! [*Recoiling.*] Stop, now!

ALBERT [*looking at her, and understanding her feelings*]. What? Can you really —? You know — we might — see one another from time to time? Nothing would please me better!

ADÈLE [*terrified*]. No, no! You mustn't! What would —? Then I —

ALBERT. Yes?

ADÈLE [*in an undertone*]. You want to take advantage of my weakness, get money from me — as before! You're not losing sight of those 150,000 francs! You've once driven me to misery and despair, but you won't a second time!

ALBERT. That thought never entered my head!

ADÈLE. Perhaps not to-day — but it would come to that!

ALBERT [*approaching her*]. You are not very kind!

ADÈLE. Go away, please!

ALBERT. I'm going, I'm going.— Good-by!

ADÈLE. Good-by! [*Stopping him on the threshold.*] Still, if you absolutely need to see me sometimes — for a good reason —?

ALBERT [*ironically*]. A good reason?

ADÈLE. Don't come here — Mama might see you, or the servants —

ALBERT. Where, then?

ADÈLE. Write me a note and arrange a meeting-place. Perhaps I'll go — I'll think it over.

ALBERT. Good! But where can I meet you?

ADÈLE. I don't know — it makes no difference.

ALBERT. The devil! Out of the question at my place. It's a tiny hole in the Batignolles district. No! I shouldn't allow my wife to be humiliated there! Perhaps — I've been thinking of setting up a ground-floor apartment. But I'm not very sure. I must decide — might see you then!? Oh, I insist on paying all the rent! Good, that's it, then! As soon as I can have you there, I'll write. You'll not have to wait long!

But you will come, won't you? Promise! Good! See you soon, then! [*He goes out.*]

ADÈLE [*after a pause*]. But will he write?

[CURTAIN.]

END OF THE PLAY

A SELECTED LIST OF DRAMATIC LITERATURE

PUBLISHED BY
STEWART & KIDD COMPANY
CINCINNATI

DRAMATIC LITERATURE

The Antigone of Sophocles

By PROF. JOSEPH EDWARD HARRY

An acting version of this most perfect of all dramas. A scholarly work in readable English. Especiallly adaptable for Colleges, Dramatic Societies, etc.

***Post Express,* Rochester:**

"He has done his work well." "Professor Harry has translated with a virile force that is almost Shakespearean." "The difficult task of rendering the choruses into English lyrical verse has been very creditably accomplished."

***Argonaut,* San Francisco:**

"Professor Harry is a competent translator not only because of his classical knowledge, but also because of a certain enthusiastic sympathy that shows itself in an unfailing choice of words and expression."

***North American,* Philadelphia:**

"Professor Harry, teacher of Greek in the Cincinnati University, has written a new metrical translation of the Antigone of Sophocles. The translation is of fine dramatic quality."

***Oregonian,* Portland:**

"A splendidly executed translation of the celebrated Greek tragedy."

***Herald,* Boston:**

"Scholars will not need to be urged to read this noteworthy piece of literary work, and we hope that many others who have no special scholarly interest will be led to its perusal."

8vo. cloth. Dignified binding.................Net, $1.00

STEWART & KIDD COMPANY

"*European Dramatists*"

By ARCHIBALD HENDERSON

Author of "George Bernard Shaw: His Life and Works."

In the present work the famous dramatic critic and biographer of Shaw has considered six representative dramatists outside of the United States, some living, some dead—Strindberg, Ibsen, Maeterlinck, Wilde, Shaw and Barker.

Velma Swanston Howard says:

"Prof. Henderson's appraisal of Strindberg is certainly the fairest, kindest and most impersonal that I have yet seen. The author has that rare combination of intellectual power and spiritual insight which casts a clear, strong light upon all subjects under his treatment."

Baltimore Evening Sun:

"Prof. Henderson's criticism is not only notable for its understanding and good sense, but also for the extraordinary range and accuracy of its information."

Jeanette L. Gilder, in the *Chicago Tribune:*

"Henderson is a writer who throws new light on old subjects."

Chicago Record Herald:

"His essays in interpretation are welcome. Mr. Henderson has a catholic spirit and writes without parochial prejudice—a thing deplorably rare among American critics of the present day. * * * One finds that one agrees with Mr. Henderson's main contentions and is eager to break a lance with him about minor points, which is only a way of saying that he is stimulating, that he strikes sparks. He knows his age thoroughly and lives in it with eager sympathy and understanding."

Providence Journal:

"Henderson has done his work, within its obvious limitations, in an exceedingly competent manner. He has the happy faculty of making his biographical treatment interesting, combining the personal facts and a fairly clear and entertaining portrait of the individual with intelligent critical comment on his artistic work."

Photogravure frontispiece, handsomely printed and bound, large 12mo........................Net, $1.50

DRAMATIC LITERATURE

At Last

You May Understand

G. B. S.

Perhaps once in a generation a figure of commanding greatness appears, one through whose life the history of his time may be read. There is but one such man to-day.

George Bernard Shaw

HIS LIFE AND WORKS

A CRITICAL BIOGRAPHY (Authorized)

By

ARCHIBALD HENDERSON, M.A.Ph.D.

Is virtually the story of the social, economic and æsthetic life of the last twenty-five years. It is a sympathetic, yet independent interpretation of the most potent individual force in society. Cultivated America will find here the key to all that is baffling and elusive in Shaw; it is a cinematographic picture of his mind with a background disclosing all the formative influences that combined to produce this universal genius.

The press of the world has united in its praise; let us send you some of the comments. It is a large demy 8vo volume cloth, gilt top, 628 pages, with 35 full page illustrations in color, photogravure and halftone and numerous pictures in the text.

$5.00 Net

STEWART & KIDD COMPANY

A FEW CRITICAL REVIEWS OF

George Bernard Shaw

HIS LIFE AND WORKS

A CRITICAL BIOGRAPHY (Authorized)

By ARCHIBALD HENDERSON, M.A., PH.D.

The Dial:

"In over five hundred pages, with an energy and carefulness and sympathy which deserve high commendation, Dr. Henderson has presented his subject from all conceivable angles."

The Bookman:

"A more entertaining narrative, whether in biography or fiction, has not appeared in recent years."

The Independent:

"Whatever George Bernard Shaw may think of his Biography the rest of the world will probably agree that Dr. Henderson has done a good job."

Boston Transcript:

"There is no exaggeration in saying it is one of the most entertaining biographies of these opening years of the Twentieth Century."

Bernard Shaw:

"You are a genius, because you are somehow susceptible to the really significant and differentiating traits and utterances of your subject."

Maurice Maeterlinck:

"You have written one of the most sagacious, most acute and most penetrating essays in the whole modern moment."

Edwin Markham:

"He stands to-day as the chief literary critic of the South, and in the very forefront of the critics of the nation."

William Lyon Phelps:

"Your critical biography of Shaw is a really great work."

Richard Burton:

"In over five hundred pages, with an energy and carefulness and sympathy which deserves high commendation, Dr. Henderson has presented his subject from all conceivable angles. * * * Intensely interesting * * * sound and brilliant, full of keen insight and happy turns of statement. * * * This service Professor Henderson's book does perform; and I incline to call it a great one."

DRAMATIC LITERATURE

Short Plays

By MARY MAC MILLAN

To fill a long-felt want. All have been successfully presented. Suitable for Women's Clubs, Girls' Schools, etc. While elaborate enough for big presentation, they may be given very simply.

Review of Reviews:

"Mary MacMillan offers 'SHORT PLAYS,' a collection of pleasant one to three-act plays for women's clubs, girls' schools, and home parlor production. Some are pure comedies, others gentle satires on women's faults and foibles. 'The Futurists,' a skit on a woman's club in the year 1882, is highly amusing. 'Entr' Act' is a charming trifle that brings two quarreling lovers together through a ridiculous private theatrical. 'The Ring' carries us gracefully back to the days of Shakespeare; and 'The Shadowed Star,' the best of the collection, is a Christmas Eve tragedy. The Star is shadowed by our thoughtless inhumanity to those who serve us and our forgetfulness of the needy. The Old Woman, gone daft, who babbles in a kind of mongrel Kiltartan, of the Shepherds, the Blessed Babe, of the Fairies, rowan berries, roses and dancing, while her daughter dies on Christmas Eve, is a splendid characterization."

Boston Transcript:

"Those who consigned the writer of these plays to solitude and prison fare evidently knew that 'needs must' is a sharp stimulus to high powers. If we find humor, gay or rich. if we find brilliant wit; if we find constructive ability joined with dialogue which moves like an arrow; if we find delicate and keen characterization, with a touch of genius in the choice of names; if we find poetic power which moves on easy wing—the gentle jailers of the writer are justified, and the gentle reader thanks their severity."

Salt Lake Tribune:

"The Plays are ten in number, all of goodly length. We prophesy great things for this gifted dramatist."

Bookseller, News Dealer & Stationer:

"The dialogue is permeated with graceful satire, snatches of wit, picturesque phraseology, and tender, often exquisite, expressions of sentiment."

Handsomely Bound. 12mo. Cloth............Net, $1.25

STEWART & KIDD COMPANY

The Gift

A POETIC DRAMA

By MARGARET DOUGLAS ROGERS

A dramatic poem in two acts, treating in altogether new fashion the world old story of Pandora, the first woman.

New Haven Times Leader:

"Well written and attractive."

Evangelical Messenger:

"A very beautifully written portrayal of the old story of Pandora."

Rochester Post Dispatch:

"There is much poetic feeling in the treatment of the subject."

Grand Rapids Herald:

"THE GIFT, dealing with this ever interesting mythological story, is a valuable addition to the dramas of the day."

St. Xavier Calendar:

"The story of Pandora is so set down as to bring out its stage possibilities. Told by Mrs. Rogers in exquisite language."

Salt Lake Tribune:

"The tale is charmingly wrought and has possibilities as a simple dramatic production, as well as being a delightful morsel of light reading."

Cincinnati Enquirer:

"The love story is delightfully told and the dramatic action of the play is swift and strong."

Buffalo Express:

"It is a delightful bit of fancy with a dramatic and poetic setting."

Boston Woman's Journal:

"Epimetheus and Pandora and her box are charmingly presented."

Worcester Gazette:

"It is absolutely refreshing to find a writer willing to risk a venture harking back to the times of the Muses and the other worthies of mythological fame. * * * The story of Pandora's box told in verse by a woman. It may be said it could not have been better written had a representative of the one who only assisted at the opening been responsible for the play."

Handsomely bound silk cloth..................Net, $1.00

DRAMATIC LITERATURE

Lucky Pehr

By AUGUST STRINDBERG

Authorized Translation by Velma Swanston Howard. An allegorical drama in five acts. Compared favorably to Barrie's "Peter Pan" and Maeterlinck's "The Blue Bird."

Rochester Post Express:

Strindberg has written many plays which might be described as realistic nightmares. But this remark does not apply to "Lucky Pehr." * * * This drama is one of the most favorable specimens of Strindberg's genius.

New York World:

"Pehr" is lucky because, having tested all things, he finds that only love and duty are true.

New York Times:

"Lucky Pehr" clothes cynicism in real entertainment instead of in gloom. And it has its surprises. Can this be August Strindberg, who ends his drama so sweetly on the note of the woman-soul, leading upward and on?

Worcester Gazette:

From a city of Ohio comes this product of Swedish fancy in most attractive attire, attesting that the possibilities of dramatic art have not entirely ceased in this age of vaudeville and moving pictures. A great sermon in altruism is preached in these pages, which we would that millions might see and hear. To those who think or would like to think, "Lucky Pehr" will prove a most readable book. * * * An allegory, it is true, but so are Æsop's Fables, the Parables of the Scriptures and many others of the most effective lessons ever given.

Boston Globe:

A popular drama. * * * There is no doubt about the book being a delightful companion in the library. In charm of fancy and grace of imagery the story may not be unfairly classed with "The Blue Bird" and "Peter Pan."

Photogravure frontispiece of Strindberg etched by Zorn. Also, a reproduction of Velma Swanston Howard's authorization.

Handsomely bound. Gilt top..................Net, $1.50

STEWART & KIDD COMPANY

Easter

(A PLAY IN THREE ACTS)

AND STORIES BY AUGUST STRINDBERG

Authorized translation by Velma Swanston Howard. In this work the author reveals a broad tolerance, a rare poetic tenderness augmented by an almost divine understanding of human frailties as marking certain natural stages in evolution of the soul.

Louisville Courier-Journal:

Here is a major key of cheerfulness and idealism —a relief to a reader who has passed through some of the author's morbid pages. * * * Some critics find in this play (Easter) less of the thrust of a distinctive art than is found in the author's more lugubrious dramas. There is indeed less sting in it. Nevertheless it has a nobler tone. It more ably fulfills the purpose of good drama—the chastening of the spectators' hearts through their participation in the suffering of the dramatic personages. There is in the play a mystical exaltation, a belief and trust in good and its power to embrace all in its beneficence, to bring all confusion to harmony.

The Nation:

Those who like the variety of symbolism which Maeterlinck has often employed—most notably in the "Bluebird"—will turn with pleasure to the short stories of Strindberg which Mrs. Howard has included in her volume. * * * They are one and all diverting on account of the author's facility in dealing with fanciful details.

Bookseller:

"Easter" is a play of six characters illustrative of human frailties and the effect of the divine power of tolerance and charity. * * * There is a symbolism, a poetic quality, a spiritual insight in the author's work that make a direct appeal to the cultured. * * *

The Dial:

One play from his (Strindberg's) third, or symbolistic period stands almost alone. This is "Easter." There is a sweet, sane, life-giving spirit about it.

Photogravure frontispiece of Strindberg etched by Zorn. Also, a reproduction of Velma Swanston Howard's authorization.

Handsomely bound. Gilt top.................Net, $1.50

DRAMATIC LITERATURE

On the Seaboard

By AUGUST STRINDBERG

The Author's greatest psychological novel. Authorized Translation by Elizabeth Clarke Westergren.

American-Scandinavian Review:

"The description of Swedish life and Swedish scenery makes one positively homesick for the Skargard and its moods.

Worcester Evening Gazette:

"Classes in Psychology in colleges, and Medical students considering Pathology would derive much information from the observations and reflections of the commissioner who holds the front of the stage whereon are presented sciences as new to the readers of to-day as were those which Frederick Bremer unfolded to the fathers and mothers of critics and observers in this first quarter of the Twentieth Century."

Detroit Tribune:

"Hans Land pronounced this novel to be the only work of art in the domain of Nietzschean morals yet written which is destined to endure."

Cincinnati Times-Star:

"It requires a book such as 'ON THE SEABOARD' to show just how profound an intellect was housed in the frame of this great Swedish writer."

New Haven Leader:

"His delineations are photographical exactness without retouching, and bear always a strong reflection of his personality."

Indianapolis News:

"The story is wonderfully built and conceived and holds the interest tight."

American Review of Reviews:

"This version is characterized by the fortunate use of idiom, a delicacy in the choice of words, and great beauty in the rendering of descriptive passages, the translation itself often attaining the melody of poetry * * * You may read and re-read it, and every reading will fascinate the mind from a fresh angle."

South Atlantic Quarterly:

"Only a most unusual man, a genius, could have written this book, and it is distinctly worth reading."

Handsomely bound, uniform with Lucky Pehr and Easter .... Net, $1.25

STEWART & KIDD COMPANY

The Hamlet Problem and Its Solution

By EMERSON VENABLE

The tragedy of Hamlet has never been adequately interpreted. Two hundred years of critical discussion has not sufficed to reconcile conflicting impressions regarding the scope of Shakespeare's design in this, the first of his great philosophic tragedies. We believe that all those students who are interested in the study of Shakespeare will find this volume of great value.

The Louisville Courier-Journal:

"Mr. Venable's Hamlet is a 'protagonist of a drama of triumphant moral achievement.' He rises through the play from an elected agent of vengeance to a man gravely impressed with 'an imperative sense of moral obligation, tragic in its depth, felt toward the world.' "

E. H. Sothern:

"Your ideas of Hamlet so entirely agree with my own that the book has been a real delight to me. I have always had exactly this feeling about the character of Hamlet. I think you have wiped away a great many cobwebs, and I believe your book will prove to be most convincing to many people who may yet be a trifle in the dark."

The Book News Monthly:

"Mr. Venable is the latest critic to apply himself to the 'Hamlet' problem, and he offers a solution in an admirably written little book which is sure to attract readers. Undeterred by the formidable names of Goethe and Coleridge, Mr. Venable pronounces untenable the theories which those great authors propounded to account for the extraordinary figure of the Prince of Denmark. * * * Mr. Venable looks in another direction for the solution of the problem. * * * The solution offered by the author is just the reverse of that proposed by Goethe. * * * From Mr. Venable's viewpoint the key to 'Hamlet' is found in the famous soliloquies, and his book is based upon a close study of those utterances which bring us within the portals of the soul of the real Hamlet. The reader with an open mind will find in Mr. Venable a writer whose breadth of view and searching thought gives weight to this competent study of the most interesting of Shakespearean problems."

16mo. Silk cloth..........................Net, $1.00

DRAMATIC LITERATURE

HOW TO WRITE

Moving Picture Plays

By W. L. GORDON

CONTENTS

What is a motion picture? How are moving pictures produced? What is necessary to write photoplays? Prices paid for plays. Kind of plays to write. Kind of plays to avoid. Single reels, double reels, etc. Preparation of manuscript. The plot and how to obtain it. Title of play. Synopsis. Cast of characters. Scenario. Leaders of Sub-Titles. Letters, Clippings, etc. What constitutes a scene. Continuity of scenes. Stage settings and properties. Entrance and exit of characters. Climax. Limitations of camera. Length of play. Review. Time required to write a play. How and where to sell plays. A complete sample play illustrating every point treated upon in the instructions. A full list of over twenty prominent film-producing companies wanting and buying plays.

The following extracts from letters of satisfied writers, addressed to the author, are very convincing and bespeak the value of this exhaustive treatise:

"Have been successful in placing three plays, and am awaiting news of two additional ones. Am certain I would never have had that much success if I had not followed your instructions."

"Your instructions entirely satisfactory. I think that any one with common sense can make a very nice income through moving picture play-writing. My first scenario has been accepted, and I desire to thank you."

"You might be interested to know that my first scenario completed according to your instructions was accepted by the Essanay Film Co."

"Instructions well worth the money. Sold my first scenario to the Edison Co."

Handsomely bound in DeLuxe Cloth...........Net, $3.00